The
Country Love
Quilt

Cheryl A. Benner
and
Rachel T. Pellman

also "The Country Bouquet Quilt"

Good Books
Intercourse, Pennsylvania 17534

Acknowledgments
Design by Cheryl Benner
Cover and color photography by Jonathan Charles
Author photo by Kenny Pellman

The Country Love Quilt
© 1989 by Good Books, Intercourse, PA 17534
International Standard Book Number:
0-934672-65-2
Library of Congress Catalog Card Number:
89-23374

Library of Congress Cataloging-in-Publication Data

Benner, Cheryl A., 1962–
   The country love quilt.

   1. Quilting — Patterns.   I. Pellman, Rachel T. (Rachel
Thomas) II. Title.
TT835.B35   1989   746.9'7041   89-23374
ISBN 0-934672-65-2

Table of Contents

7 The Country Love Quilt

8 How to Begin
8 Applique Quilts
8 Preparing Background Fabric for Appliqueing
9 Making Templates
9 Appliqueing
10 Assembling the Appliqued Quilt Top
10 Quilting on Applique Quilts
10 Marking Quilting Designs
11 Quilting
11 Binding
12 To Display Quilts
12 Signing and Dating Quilts
13 Cutting Layouts for The Country Love Quilt
13 Fabric Requirements
14 Assembly Instructions
15 Country Love Quilt Applique Templates
55 Country Love Quilt Applique Layout
91 Country Love Quilt Pillow Throw Applique Layout
93 Country Love Quilt Quilting Template

117 The Country Bouquet Quilt

118 Assembly Instructions
121 Fabric Requirements
123 Country Bouquet Quilt Applique Templates
131 Country Bouquet Quilt Applique Layout
145 Country Bouquet Quilt Pillow Throw Applique Layout
159 Country Bouquet Quilt Quilting Template
191 About the Old Country Store
192 About the Authors

The Country Love Quilt

The Country Love Quilt follows in the tradition of the popular Country Bride quilt. Also created by the Old Country Store staff, Country Love has a flourish and fullness reminiscent of the Victorian era. A combination of old and new, the Country Love quilt is based on the traditional Center Diamond motif; its center diamond section is covered with lavish applique work. The four triangles which complete the square continue the theme of hearts, ribbons and roses. The center boasts one dozen roses; each triangle and the pillow throw section add six more. The scalloped border is emphasized with an appliqued scallop highlighted by a rose at each point.

This is a quilt for the dedicated quiltmaker. The applique is extensive and many pieces overlap. Because it is done following the Center Diamond motif, much of the applique needs to be worked on a large section of background fabric. And, when the applique work is completed, the quilting lines are abundant and close. The effort is worthwhile—the finished quilt is magnificent. This is a quilt to be made as an heirloom. The love and time stitched into it will be treasured from generation to generation.

With the Country Love quilt, we offer another original applique design—The Country Bouquet. Country Bouquet has five applique patches strewn with flowers. These alternate with more subdued patches where quilting lines whisper a similar floral motif surrounded by appliqued hearts. This profusion of flowers and quilting is all contained within a generously quilted scalloped border. Country Bouquet celebrates the freshness of new life and the delicacy of springtime flowers.

The types of fabric you choose will greatly affect the overall look of your quilt. The original Country Love uses large florals in pinks and blacks, giving it a Victorian flavor in keeping with its design. However, it can be equally stunning in soft muted fabrics.

Country Bouquet was originally done in soft peach, blue and green. This gentle combination creates a restful, peaceful quilt. The design can lend itself equally well to bright, vibrant colors.

How to Begin

Read the following instructions thoroughly before beginning work on your quilt.

All fabrics should be washed before cutting. This will pre-shrink and also test them for colorfastness. If the fabric is not colorfast after one washing, either repeat the washings until the water remains clear or replace the cloth with another fabric. If fabrics are wrinkled after washing and drying they should be ironed before use.

Fabrics suitable for quilting are generally lightweight, tightly woven cotton and cotton/polyester blends. They should not unravel easily and should not hold excessive wrinkles when squeezed and released. Because of the hours of time required to make a quilt, it is worth investing in high quality fabrics.

Fabric requirements given here are for standard 45″ wide fabric. If wider or more narrow fabrics are used, calculate the variations needed.

All seams are sewn using ¼″ seam allowances. Measurements given include seam allowances, *except* for applique pieces (See "How to Applique" section).

Applique Quilts

Preparing Background Fabric for Appliqueing

When purchasing fabric to be used for background and borders, it is best to buy the total amount needed from one bolt of fabric. This will assure that all the patches and borders will be the same shade. Dye lots can vary significantly from bolt to bolt of fabric, and those differences are emphasized when placed next to each other in a quilt top.

Cutting diagrams are shown to make the most efficient use of fabric. Label each piece when it is cut. Mark the right and wrong sides of the fabric as well.

To indicate the placement of applique pieces on the background piece, trace the applique design lightly on the right side of the background fabric. Even though the applique pieces will be laid over these markings and stitched in place, it is important to mark these lines as lightly as possible to avoid show-through. Center the applique designs on the background sections. The placement of the applique on the pillow throw is an exception to that rule. That applique should be centered from side to side but should be placed nearer the top of the quilt so that there is extra fullness for tucking the quilt under the pillows. The space from the top of the pillow throw section to the highest point of the applique design should measure about 10 inches.

Making Templates

Make templates from pattern pieces printed in this book, using material that will not wear along the edges from repeated tracing. Cardboard is suitable for pieces being traced only a few times. Plastic lids or the sides of plastic cartons work well for templates that will be used repeatedly. Quilt supply shops and art supply stores carry sheets of plastic that function well for template-making.

Precision begins with marking. First, test the template you have made against the original printed pattern for accuracy. The applique templates are given in their actual size, without seam allowances. Trace them that way. They should then be traced on the right side of the fabric, but spaced far enough apart so that they can be cut approximately ¼" outside the marked line. The traced line is the fold line indicating the exact shape of the applique piece. Since these lines will be on the right side of the fabric and will be on the folded edge, markings should be as light as possible.

Each applique piece needs to be traced separately (rather than having the fabric doubled) so the fold line is marked on each one. However, since some of the pieces face in opposite directions, half should be traced in one direction and the other half should be traced in the opposite direction (see illustration).

Appliqueing

Begin by appliqueing the cut-out fabric pieces, one at a time, over the placement lines drawn onto the background fabric pieces. Be alert to the sequence in which the pieces are applied, so that sections which overlie each other are done in proper order. For example, when doing the center diamond section of the Country Love quilt, most leaves will need to be done first. Roses overlay leaves and hearts overlay roses. In cases where a portion of an applique piece is covered by another, the section being covered does not need to be stitched, since it will be held in place by the stitches of the section that overlies it.

Appliqueing is not difficult, but it does require patience and precision. The best applique work has perfectly smooth curves and sharply defined points. To achieve this, stitches must be very small and tight. First, pin the piece being appliqued to the outline on the background piece. Using thread that matches the piece being applied, stitch the piece to the background section, folding the seam allowance under to the traced line on the applique piece. Fold under only a tiny section at a time.

The applique stitch is a running stitch going through the background fabric and emerging to catch only a few threads of the appliqued piece along the folded line. The needle should re-enter the background piece for the next stitch at almost the same place it emerged, creating a stitch so small that it is almost

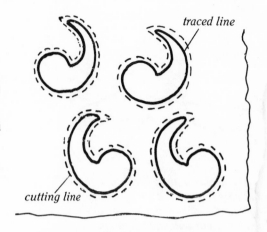

traced line

cutting line

Applique templates should be traced on the right side of the fabric but spaced far enough apart so they can be cut approximately ¼" outside the marked line.

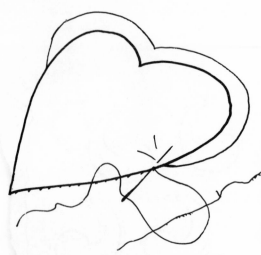

The applique stitch is a tiny, tight stitch that goes through the background fabric and emerges to catch only a few threads of the appliqued piece along the fold line.

invisible along the edge of the appliqued piece. Stitches on the underside of the background fabric should be about ⅛″ long.

To form sharp points, fold in one side and stitch almost to the end of the point. Fold in the opposite side to form the point and push the excess seam allowance under with the point of the needle. Stitch tightly.

To form smooth curves, clip along the curves to the fold line. Fold under while stitching, using the needle to push under the seam allowances.

After appliqueing is completed, embroidery work will be required for the stems, and rose centers. Matching or contrasting thread may be used.

Assembling the Appliqued Quilt Top

When all applique work is completed, the patches are ready to be assembled. See the diagrams on pages 14 and 119.

Partial assembly of the Country Love patches will be required to complete the applique work. The entire center section will need to be assembled to applique the trailing vine. Most of the vine does not extend over onto the border. However, at the corners the roses will extend to the borders. Because it is easier to applique smaller sections, assemble the center section and mark as much of the applique as possible. Applique these leaves. When this is completed, add the appliqued border sections and finish the marking and applique. This will allow you to do a minimum amount of applique while contending with the entire bulk of the quilt.

Quilting on Applique and Pieced Quilts

Quilting lines are marked on the surface of the quilt top. Markings should be as light as possible so they are easily seen for quilting, yet do not distract when the quilting is completed.

Marking Quilting Designs

Quilting designs are marked on the surface of the quilt top. A lead pencil provides a thin line and, if used with very little pressure, creates markings that are easily seen for quilting, yet do not distract when the quilt is completed. There are numerous marking pencils on the market, as well as chalk markers. Test whatever you choose on a scrap piece of fabric to be sure it performs as promised. Remember, quilting lines are not opaqued by quilting stitches, so the lines should be light or removable.

Patterns for quilting designs are included in this book. Since most spread over several pages, they will need to be assembled before they can be used.

Quilting

A quilt consists of three layers—the back or underside of the quilt, the batting, and top, which is the appliqued layer. Quilting stitches follow a decorative pattern, piercing through all three layers of the quilt "sandwich" and holding it together.

Many quilters prefer to stretch their quilts into large quilting frames. These are built so that the finished area of the quilt can be rolled up as work on it progresses. This type of frame allows space for several quilters to work on the same quilt and is used at quilting bees. Smaller hoops can be used to quilt small sections at a time. If you use one of the smaller frames, be sure that the three layers of the quilt are stretched and thoroughly basted together to keep the layers together without puckering.

The quilting stitch is a simple running stitch. Quilting needles are called "betweens" and are shorter than "sharps," which are regular hand-sewing needles. The higher the number, the smaller the needle. Many quilters prefer a size 8 or 9 needle.

Quilting is done with a single strand of quilting thread. The thread is knotted and the needle is inserted through the top layer about one inch away from the point where quilting will begin emerging on a marked quilting line. The knot is gently tugged through the fabric so it is hidden between the layers. The needle then re-enters the quilt top, going through all layers of the quilt.

The quilter's one hand remains under the quilt to feel when the needle has successfully penetrated all layers and to help guide the needle back up to the surface. The upper hand receives the needle and repeats the process. A series of as many as five stitches can be "stacked" on the needle before pulling the thread through. When working curves, fewer stitches can be stacked. Quilting stitches should be pulled taut but not so tight as to pucker the fabric. When the entire length of thread has been used, the stitching should be reinforced with a tiny back-stitch. The needle is then reinserted in the top layer, pushed through for a long stitch, and then pulled out and clipped.

The goal in quilting is to have straight, even stitches that are of equal length on both the top and bottom of the quilt. This is best achieved with hours of practice.

A quilt is a sandwich of three layers—the quilt back, batting and the quilt top—all held together by the quilting stitches.

Binding

The final stage in completing a quilt is the binding, which finishes the quilt's raw edge. When binding the edges of a scalloped quilt, it is best to cut the binding strips on the bias. This allows more flex and stretch around curves. To cut on the bias, cut the fabric at a 45 degree angle to the straight of grain.

A double thickness of binding on the edge of the quilt gives it additional strength and durability. To create a double binding, cut the binding strips 2-2½″ wide. Sew strips together to form a continuous length of binding. For a scalloped-edge quilt, this length will need to equal the two lengths plus the bottom edge of the quilt. The upper edge is straight.

To sew binding on a scalloped edge, baste the raw edges of the quilt together. Mark the scallops. Sew the binding along the marked edge. Trim the scallops even with the edge of the binding. Wrap the binding around to the back, enclosing the raw edges and covering the stitch line. Slipstitch in place with thread that matches the color of the binding fabric.

To Display Quilts

Wall quilts can be hung in various ways. One is simply to tack the quilt directly to the wall. However, this is potentially damaging to both the quilt and wall. Except for a permanent hanging, this is probably not the best way.

Another option is to hang the quilt like a painting. To do this, make a narrow sleeve from matching fabric and hand-sew it to the upper edge of the quilt along the base. Insert a dowel rod through the sleeve and hang the rod by wire or nylon string.

The quilt can also be hung on a frame. This method requires Velcro or fabric to be attached to the frame itself. If you use Velcro, staple one side of it to the frame. Hand-sew the opposite Velcro on the edges of the quilt, then attach it carefully to the Velcro on the frame. If fabric is attached to the frame, the quilt is then hand-stitched to the frame itself.

Quilts can also be mounted inside Plexiglas by a professional framery. This method, often reserved for antique quilts, provides an acid-free, dirt-free and, with special Plexiglas, a sun-proof environment for your quilt.

Signing and Dating Quilts

To preserve history for future generations, sign and date the quilts you make. Include your initials and the year the quilt was made. This data is usually added discreetly in a corner of the quilt. It can be embroidered or quilted among the quilting designs. Another alternative is to stitch or write the information on a separate piece of fabric and hand-stitch it to the back of the quilt. Whatever method you choose, this is an important part of finishing a quilt.

The Country Love Quilt
Cutting Lay-out for Queen-size or Double-size Quilt

Final size — approximately 92″ × 108″
Measurements include seam allowances

Total yardage for quilt top — 8¾ yards
Total yardage for quilt back — 6¼ yards
plus 12″ width left from cutting side borders.

Quilt Back (6¼″ yards) plus 12″ left from cutting borders on front

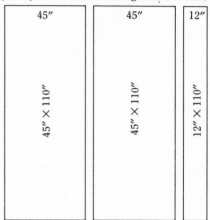

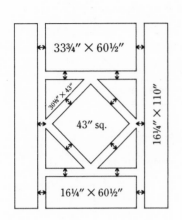

Side Borders
112½″ × 45″ (3⅛ yards)

Side Border — 16¼″ × 110″

Side Border — 16¼″ × 110″

Quilt Back — 12″ left

Center Diamond, Corner Triangles, Pillow Throw, Bottom Border (5¾ yards = 207″)

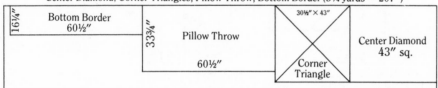

Yardage for Applique

If you decide to use large prints, look carefully at the printed area. There may be open spaces that could result in vacant sections, in which case you need to calculate that loss and purchase additional fabrics.

Bows and Hearts: (floral print) — ¾ yard

Hearts: (solid fabric) — ¼ yard

Leaves: (solid fabric) — 1¾ yards
(print fabric) — ¼ yard

Roses: ⅓ yard each of four fabrics. Choose 2 solids and 2 printed fabrics. (One solid is the same as solid fabric of hearts.) Each single rose is constructed of 4 fabrics — 2 prints and 2 solids. Placement of these four fabrics within roses may vary. When clustered together, rose shape is more clearly defined if identical fabrics are not overlapping.

Bias tape: Used on border scallop

Assembly Instructions for the Country Love Quilt
Queen-size/Double-size

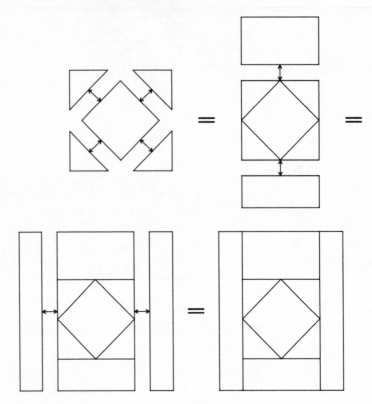

Country Love Quilt Applique Templates

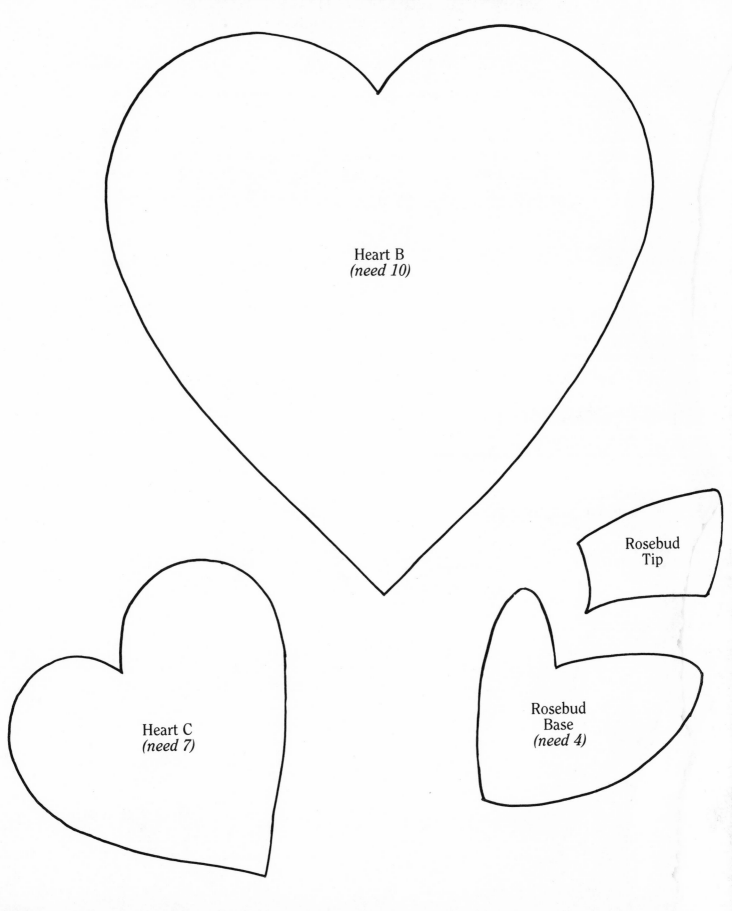

Heart B
(need 10)

Heart C
(need 7)

Rosebud
Tip

Rosebud
Base
(need 4)

Heart A
(need 1)

Country Love Quilt Applique Templates

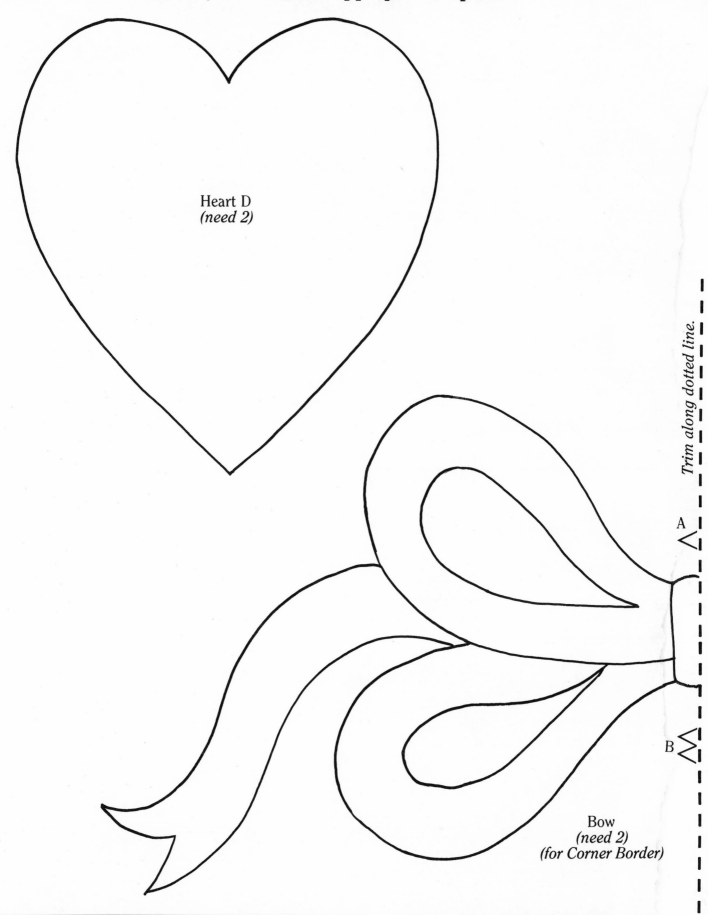

Heart D
(need 2)

Bow
(need 2)
(for Corner Border)

A

B

Trim along dotted line.

Country Love Quilt Applique Template

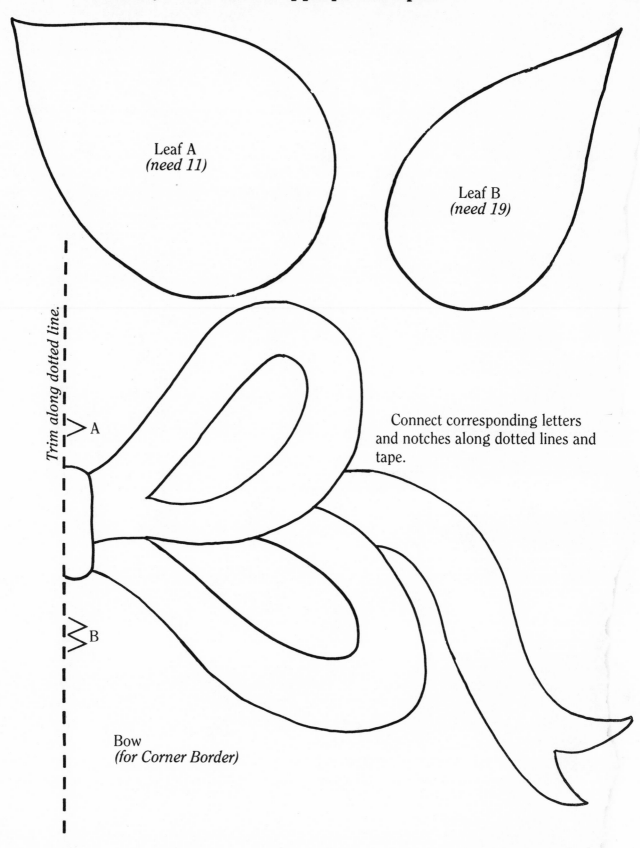

Leaf A
(need 11)

Leaf B
(need 19)

Trim along dotted line.

A

Connect corresponding letters and notches along dotted lines and tape.

B

Bow
(for Corner Border)

Country Love Quilt Applique Template

Pillow Throw Bow

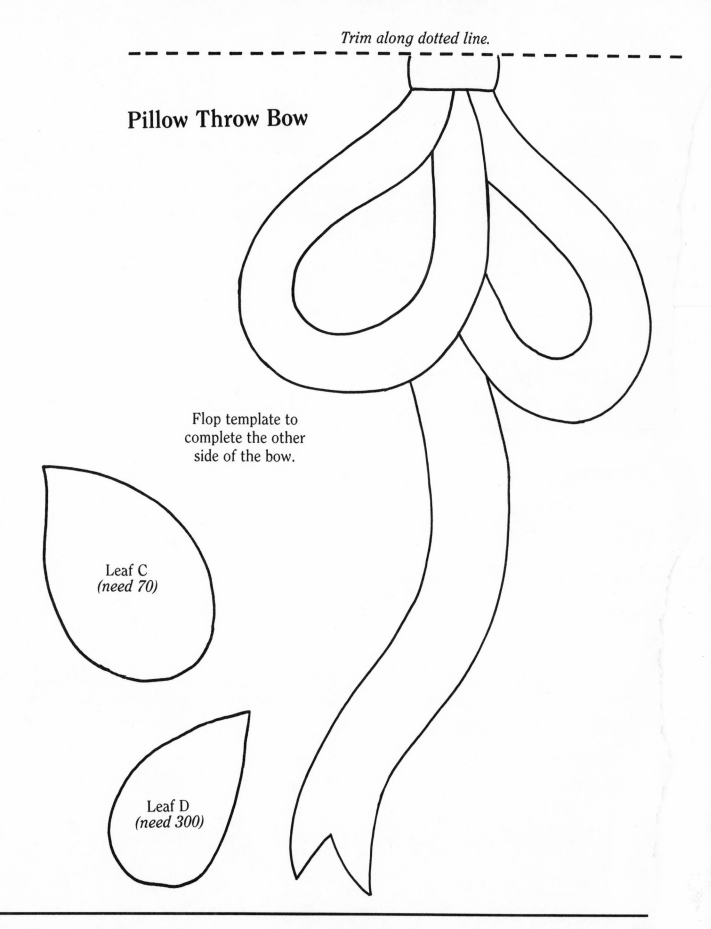

Flop template to
complete the other
side of the bow.

Leaf C
(need 70)

Leaf D
(need 300)

Tiny Single Rose

(need 4)

(for corners of the Trailing Vine.)

Note: Some rose templates will need to be cut facing the opposite direction.

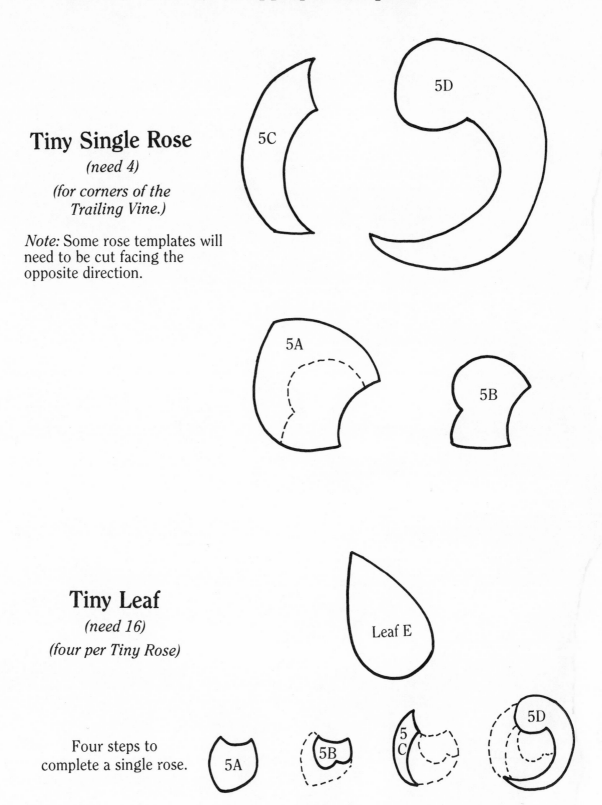

Tiny Leaf

(need 16)

(four per Tiny Rose)

Four steps to complete a single rose.

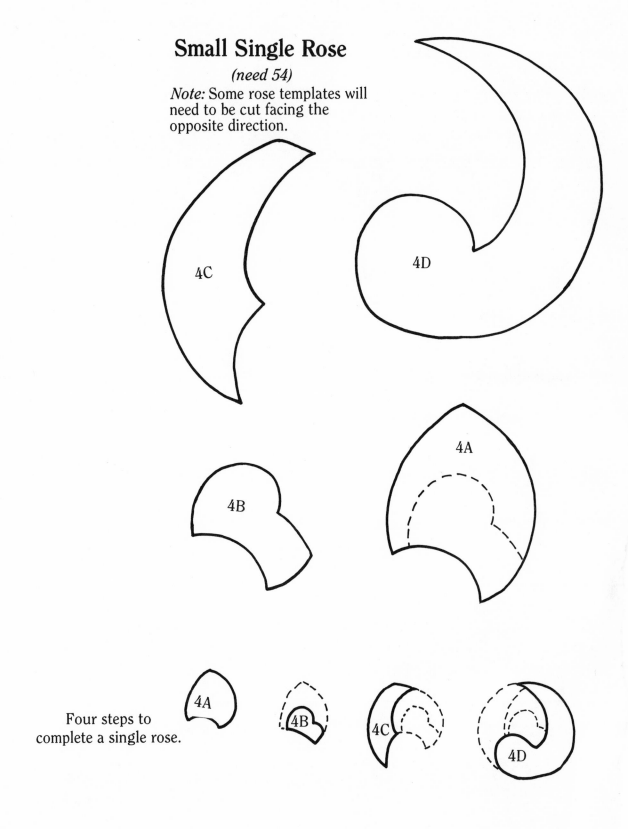

Small Single Rose

(need 54)

Note: Some rose templates will
need to be cut facing the
opposite direction.

4C

4D

4B

4A

4A

4B

4C

4D

Four steps to
complete a single rose.

Country Love Quilt Applique Templates

Medium Single Rose
(need 20)

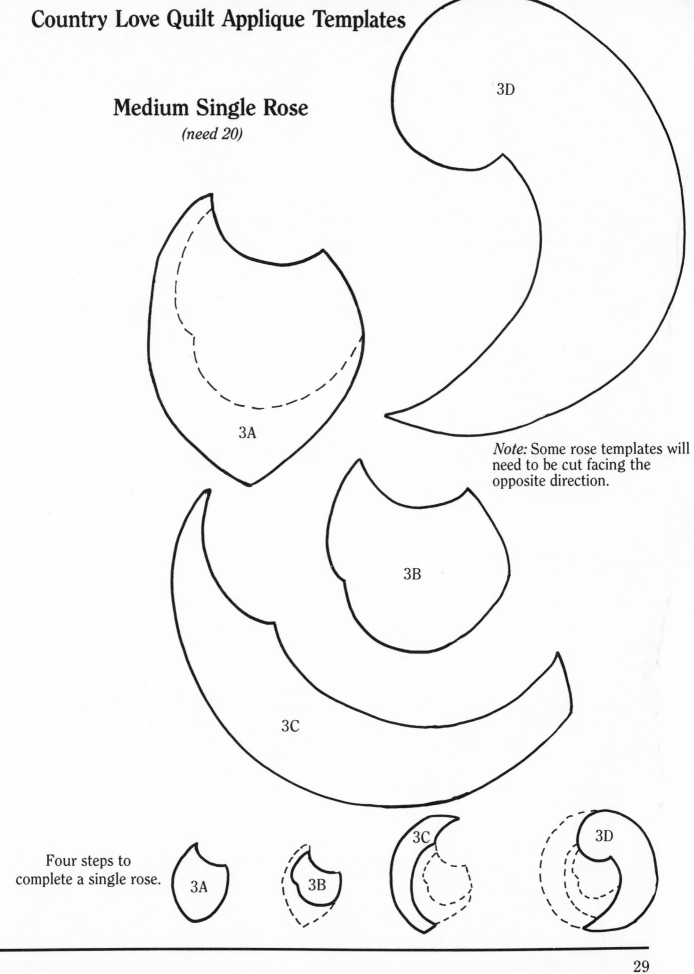

Note: Some rose templates will need to be cut facing the opposite direction.

Four steps to complete a single rose.

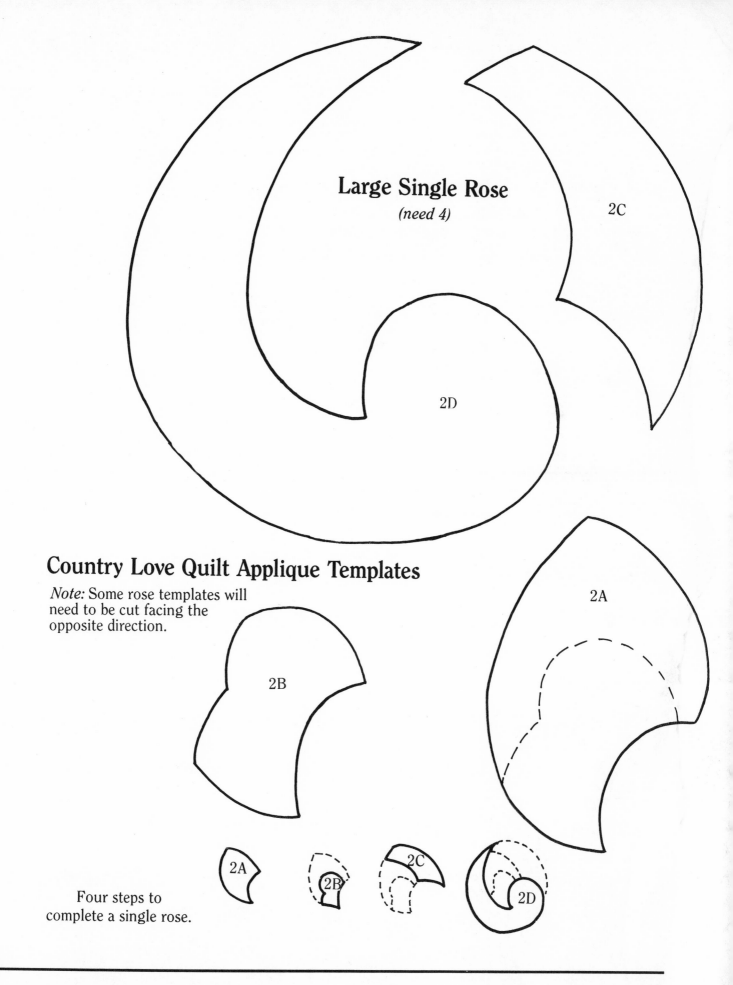

Large Single Rose
(need 4)

2C

2D

Country Love Quilt Applique Templates

Note: Some rose templates will
need to be cut facing the
opposite direction.

2B

2A

2A

2B

2C

2D

Four steps to
complete a single rose.

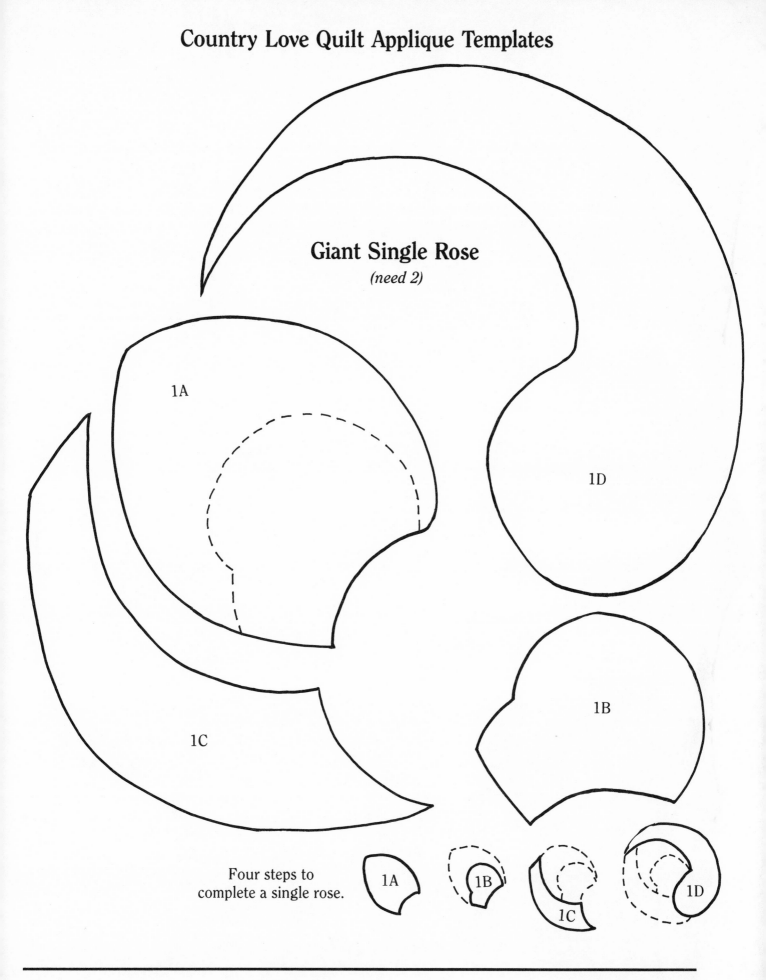

Giant Single Rose

(need 2)

1A

1D

1C

1B

Four steps to
complete a single rose.

1A   1B   1C   1D

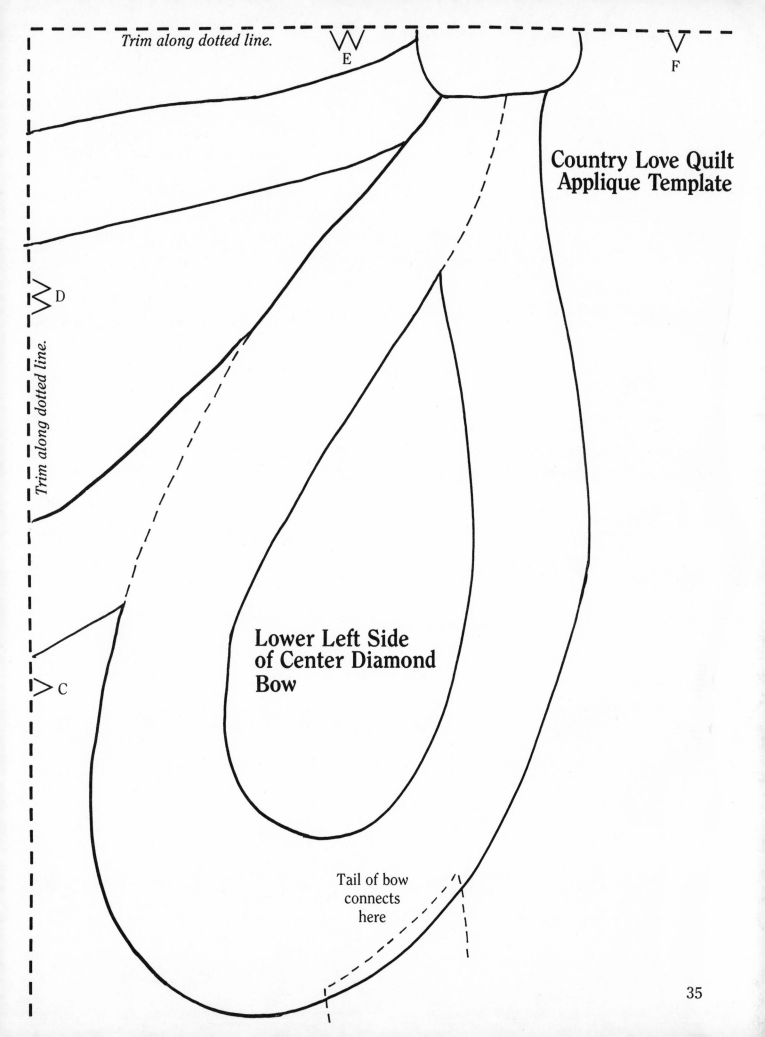

Trim along dotted line.

W
E

V
F

**Country Love Quilt
Applique Template**

W
D

Trim along dotted line.

V
C

**Lower Left Side
of Center Diamond
Bow**

Tail of bow
connects
here

35

Country Love Quilt Applique Template

**Upper Left Side of
Center Diamond Bow**

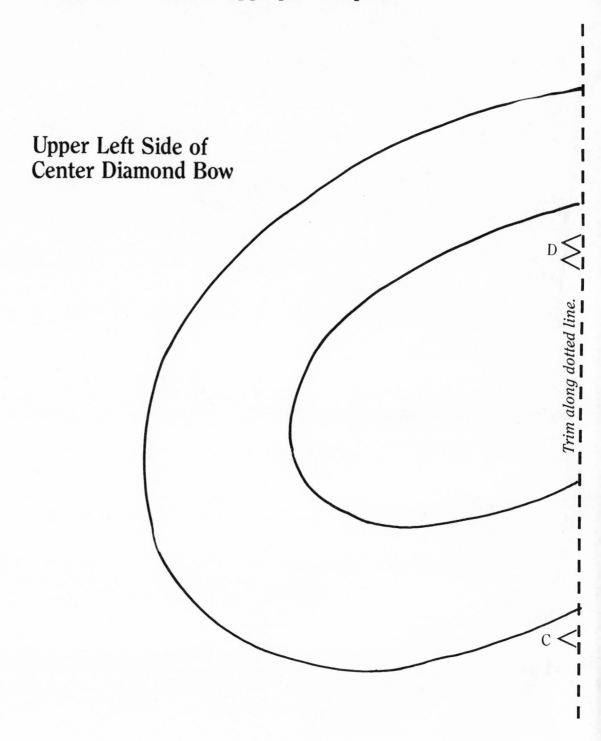

D

C

Trim along dotted line.

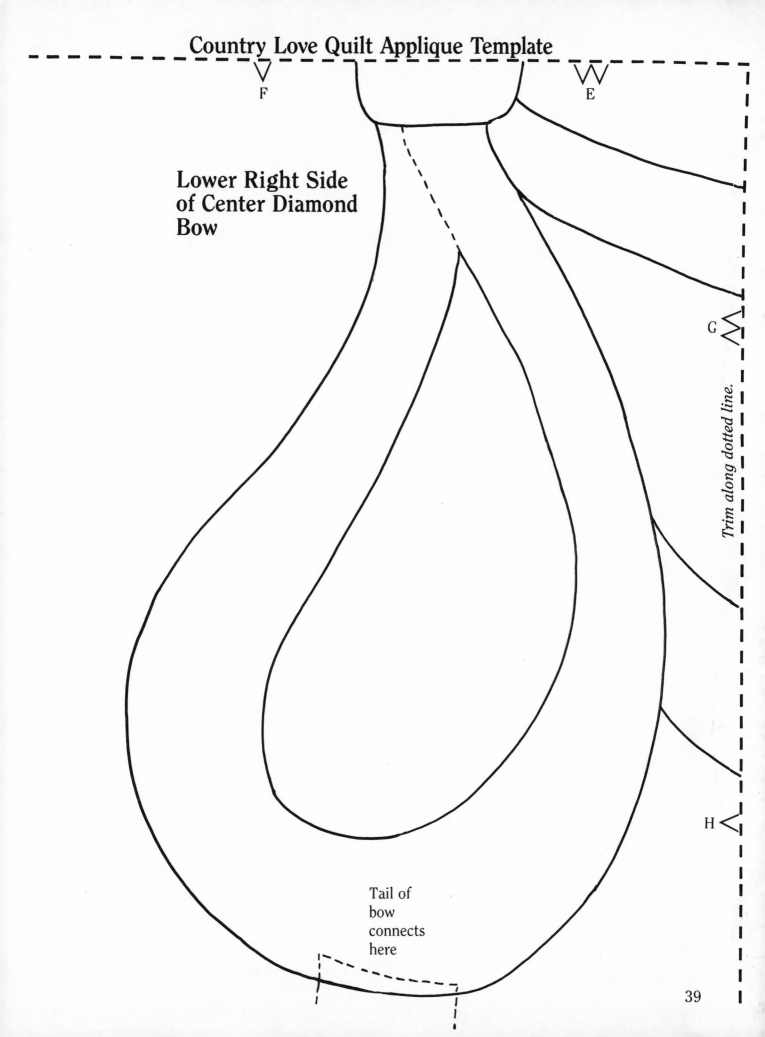

Country Love Quilt Applique Template

F

E

Lower Right Side of Center Diamond Bow

G

Trim along dotted line.

H

Tail of
bow
connects
here

Country Love Quilt Applique Template

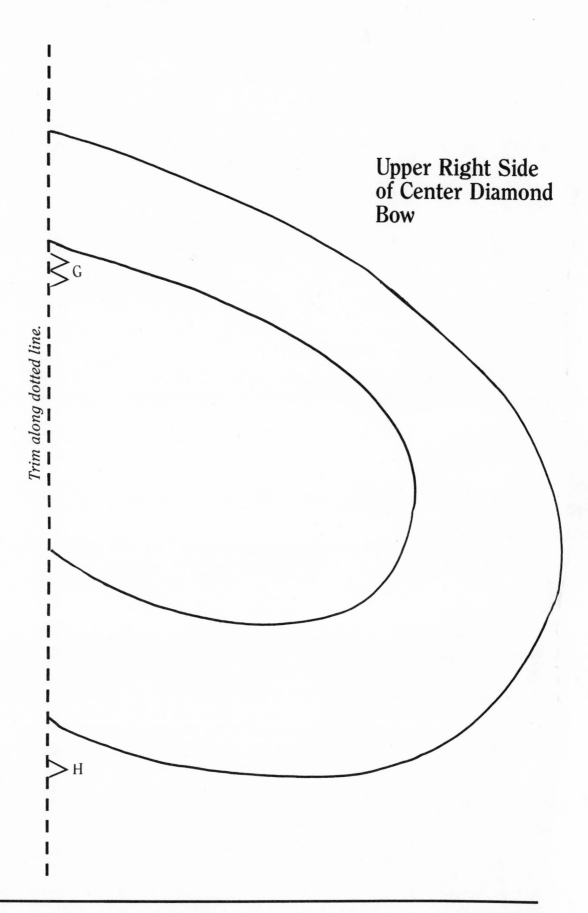

Upper Right Side of Center Diamond Bow

Trim along dotted line.

G

H

Country Love Quilt Applique Templates

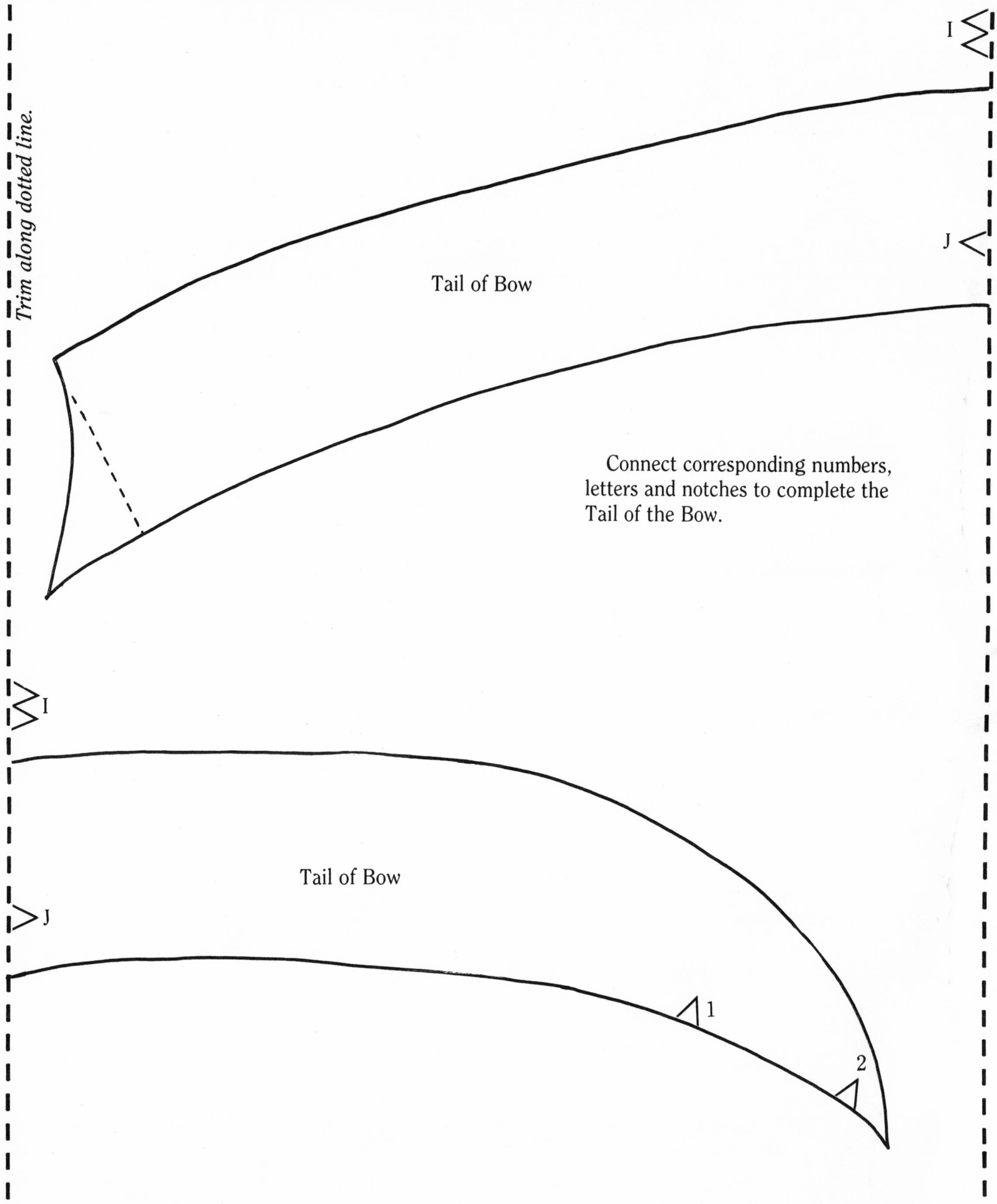

Trim along dotted line.

I

J

Tail of Bow

Connect corresponding numbers,
letters and notches to complete the
Tail of the Bow.

I

Tail of Bow

J

1

2

Country Love Quilt Applique Templates

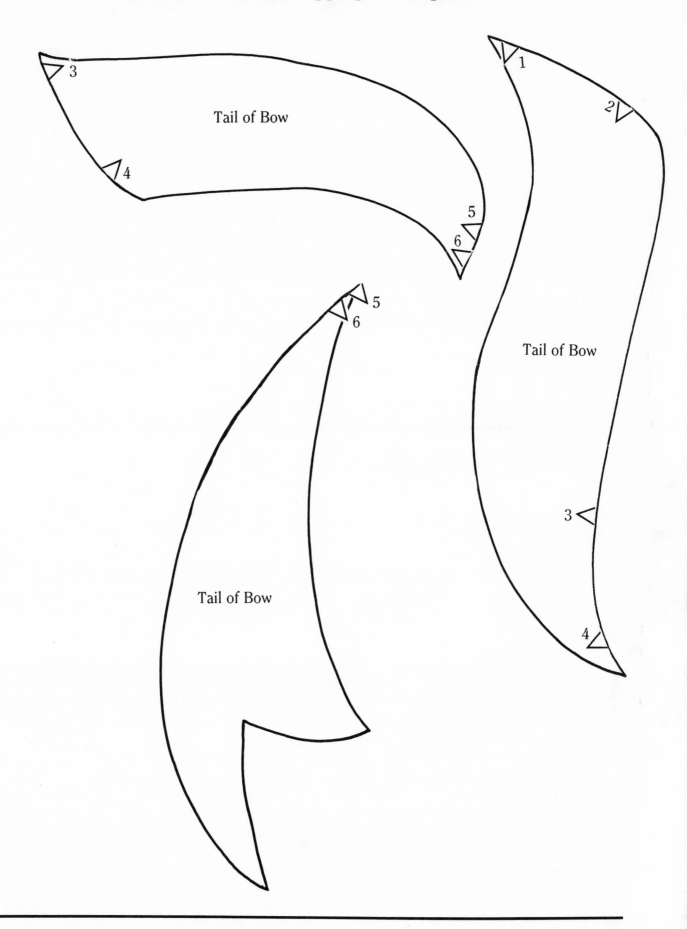

Tail of Bow

3

4

Tail of Bow

5

6

1

2

Tail of Bow

3

4

5

6

Trim along dotted line.

C

W
D

Scallop Border

Connect corresponding letters
and notches along dotted lines and
tape.

Completed template will look like
this:

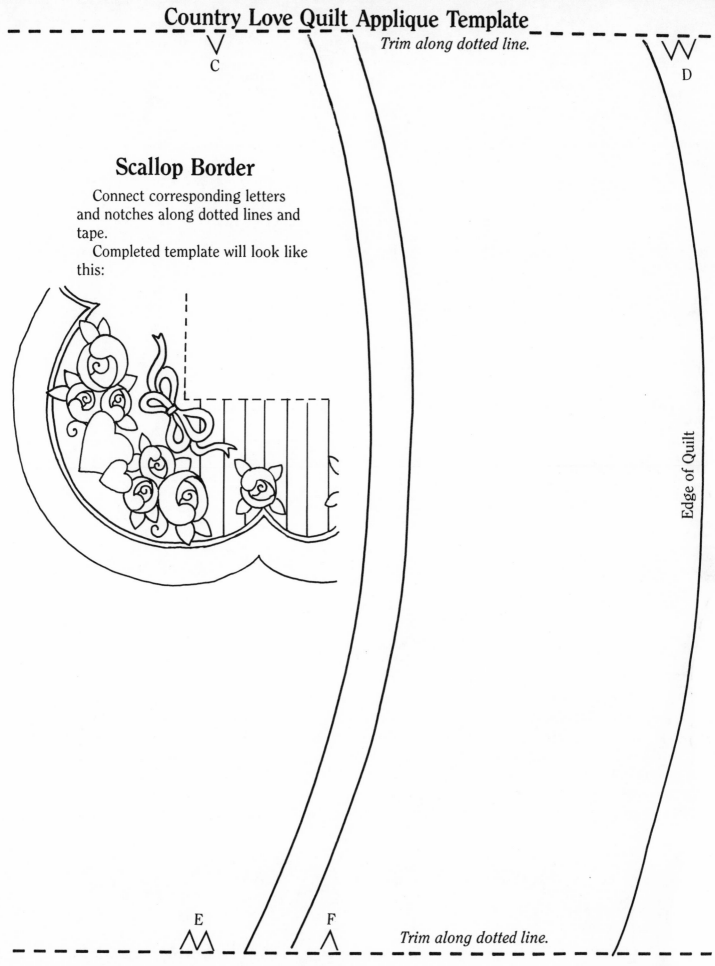

Edge of Quilt

E

F

Trim along dotted line.

Country Love Quilt Applique Template

Scallop Border

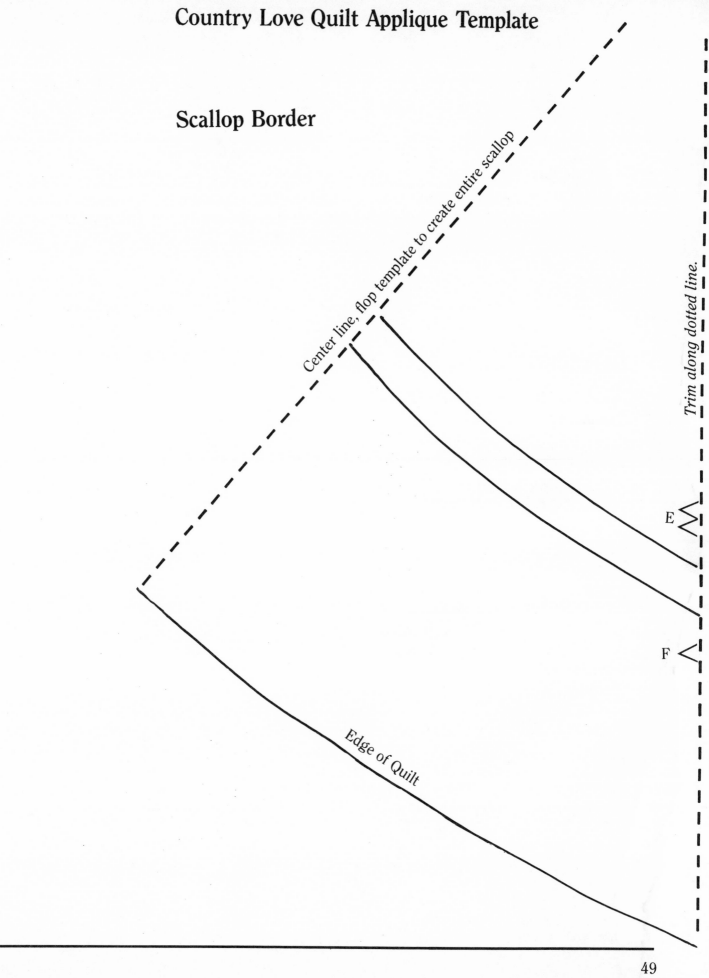

Center line, flop template to create entire scallop

Trim along dotted line.

E

F

Edge of Quilt

Country Love Quilt Applique Template
Scallop Border

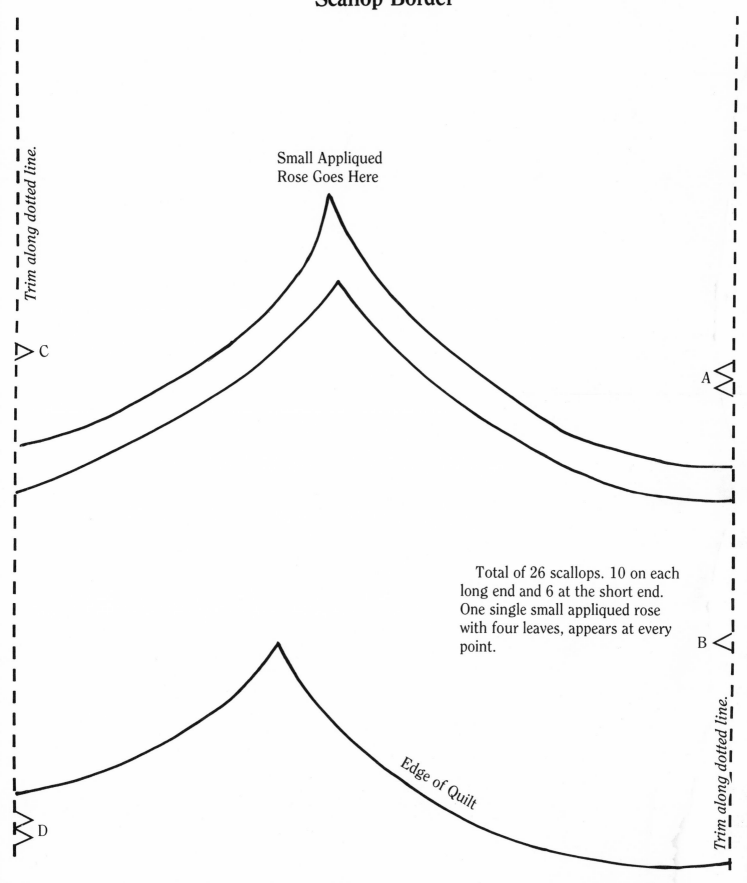

Small Appliqued
Rose Goes Here

Trim along dotted line.

C

A

B

Total of 26 scallops. 10 on each
long end and 6 at the short end.
One single small appliqued rose
with four leaves, appears at every
point.

D

Edge of Quilt

Trim along dotted line.

Country Love Quilt Applique Template
Scallop Border

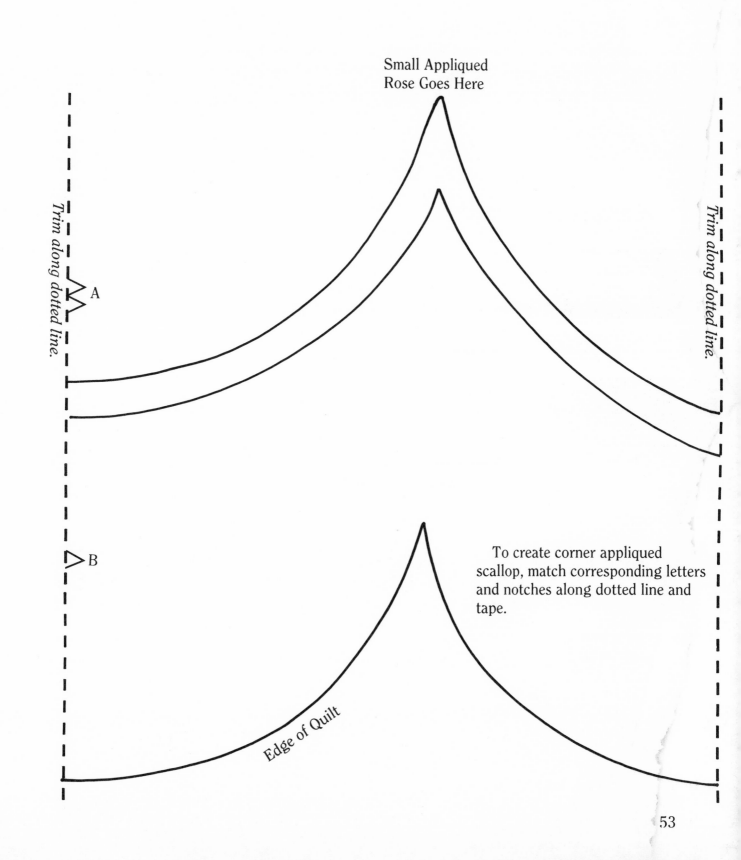

Small Appliqued
Rose Goes Here

Trim along dotted line.

Trim along dotted line.

A

B

To create corner appliqued
scallop, match corresponding letters
and notches along dotted line and
tape.

Edge of Quilt

Country Love Quilt Applique Layout
Center Diamond

To create center diamond layout, connect corresponding letters and notches along dotted lines and tape. Completed layout will look like this:

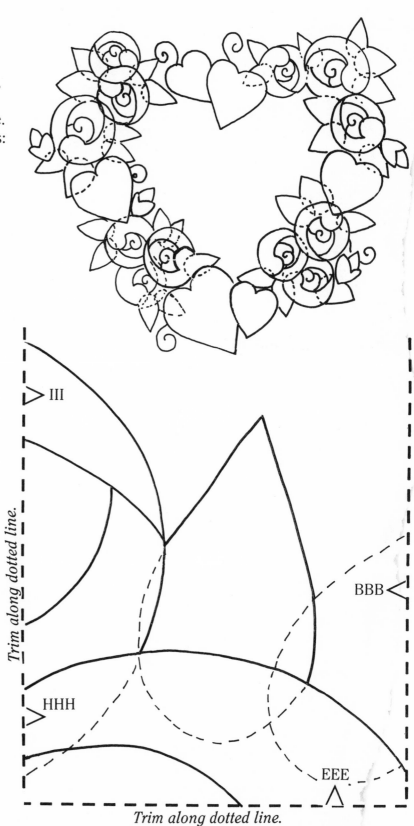

Trim along dotted line.

III

BBB

HHH

EEE

Trim along dotted line.

Country Love Quilt Applique Layout
Center Diamond

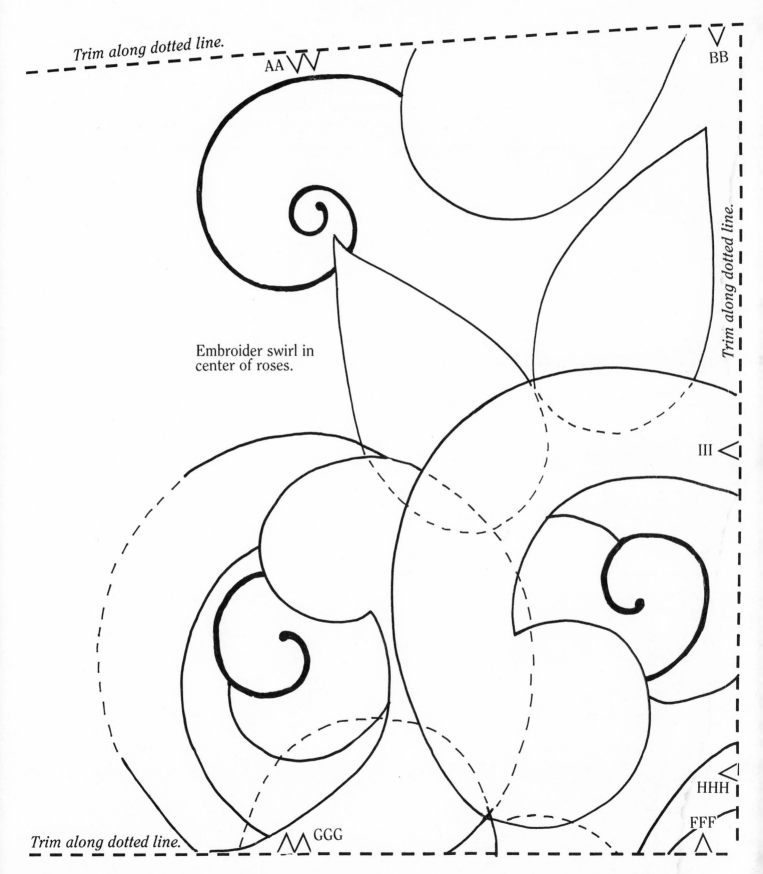

Trim along dotted line.

AA

BB

Trim along dotted line.

Embroider swirl in
center of roses.

III

HHH

FFF

Trim along dotted line.

GGG

Country Love Quilt Applique Layout
Center Diamond

Trim along dotted line.

AA

BB

CC

DD

Trim along dotted line.

Country Love Quilt Applique Layout
Center Diamond

GGG

FFF

Embroider swirl in
center of rose

Trim along dotted line.

EEE

DDD

CCC

Trim along dotted line.

61

Country Love Quilt Applique Layout
Center Diamond

Trim along dotted line.

BBB

AAA

Trim along dotted line.

ZZ

WW

XX

Trim along dotted line.

Country Love Quilt Applique Layout

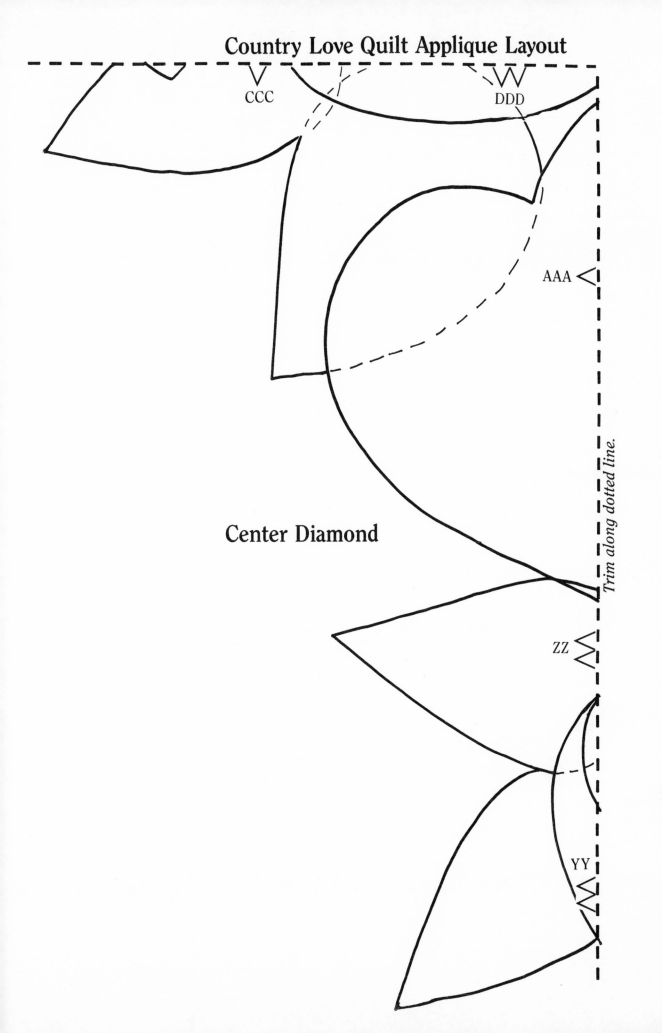

CCC

DDD

AAA

Center Diamond

Trim along dotted line.

ZZ

YY

Country Love Quilt Applique Layout

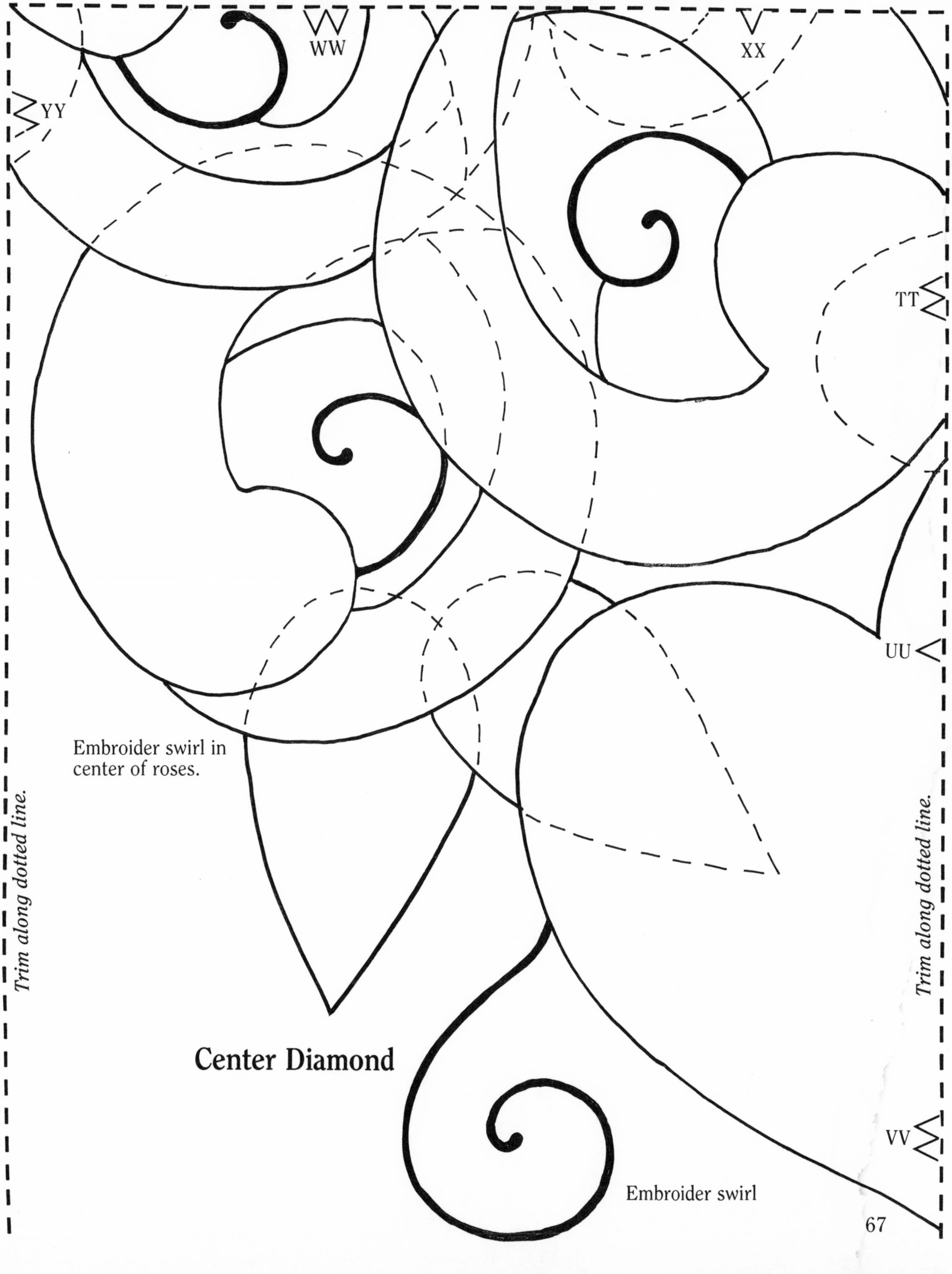

WW
XX
YY
TT
UU
VV
Trim along dotted line.
Trim along dotted line.
Embroider swirl in center of roses.
Center Diamond
Embroider swirl

Country Love Quilt Applique Layout
Center Diamond

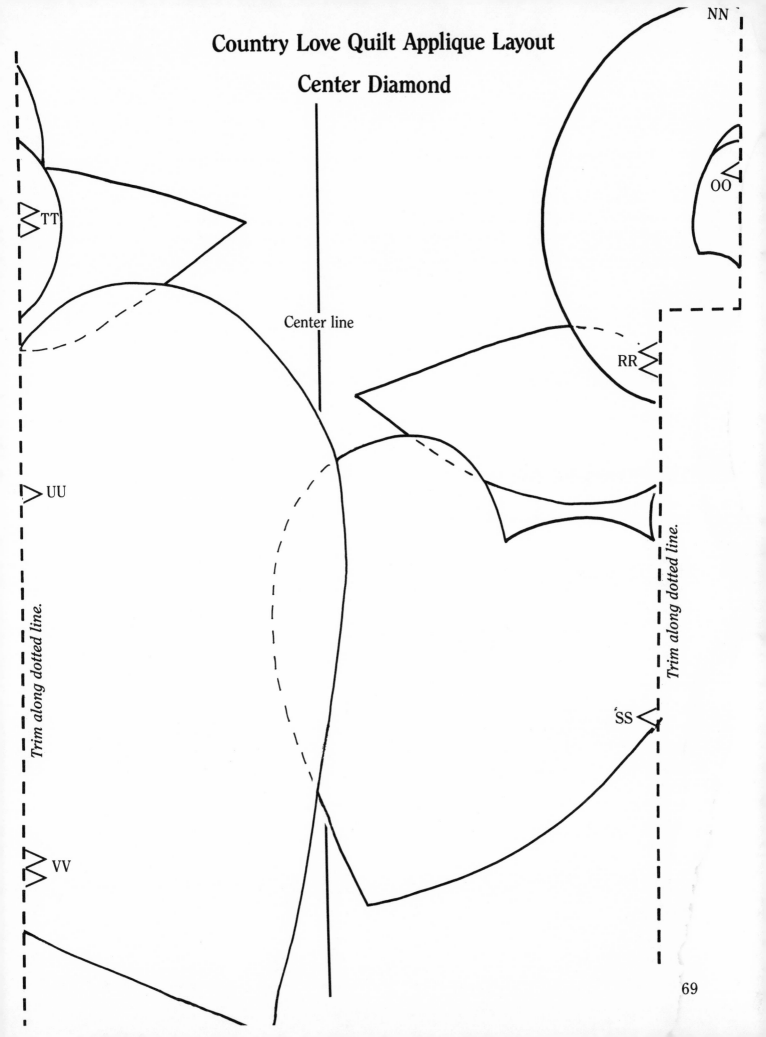

NN

OO

TT

Center line

RR

UU

Trim along dotted line.

Trim along dotted line.

SS

VV

Country Love Quilt Applique Layout

Center Diamond

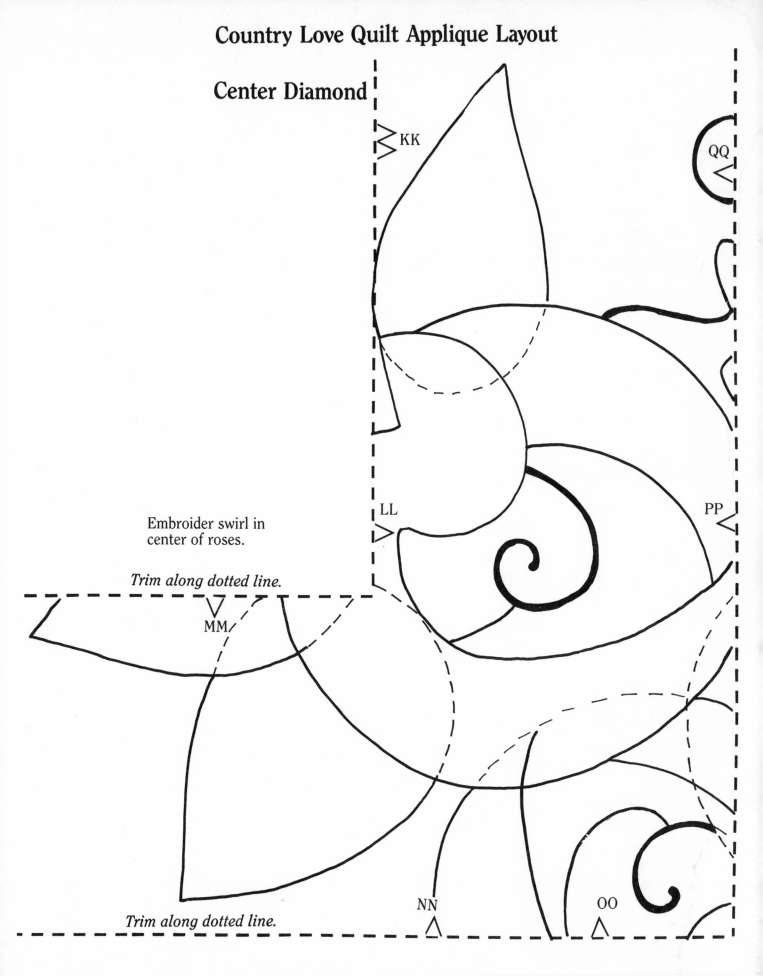

Embroider swirl in center of roses.

Trim along dotted line.

KK

LL

MM

QQ

PP

NN

OO

Trim along dotted line.

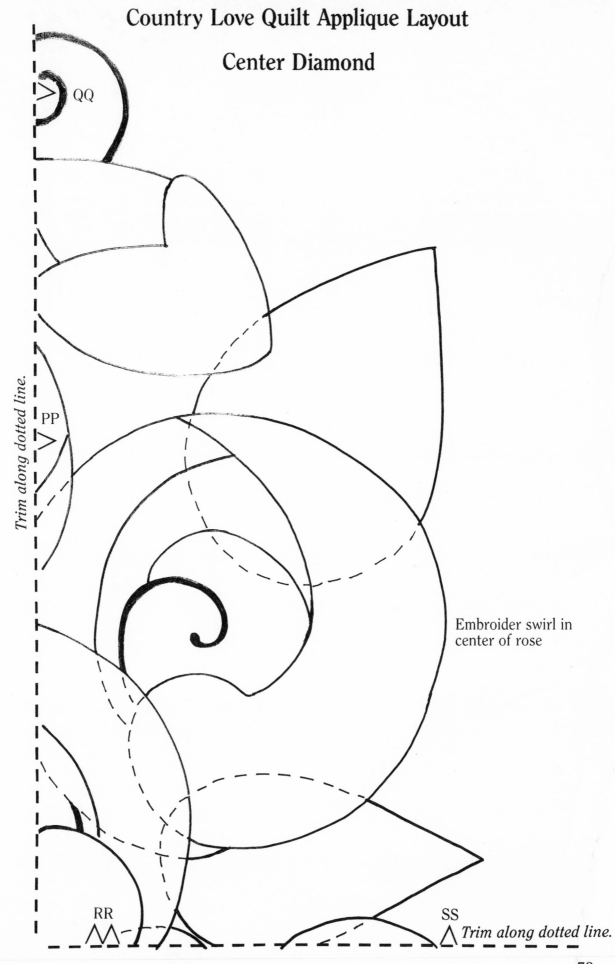

QQ

Trim along dotted line.

PP

Embroider swirl in
center of rose

RR

SS *Trim along dotted line.*

Country Love Quilt Applique Layout

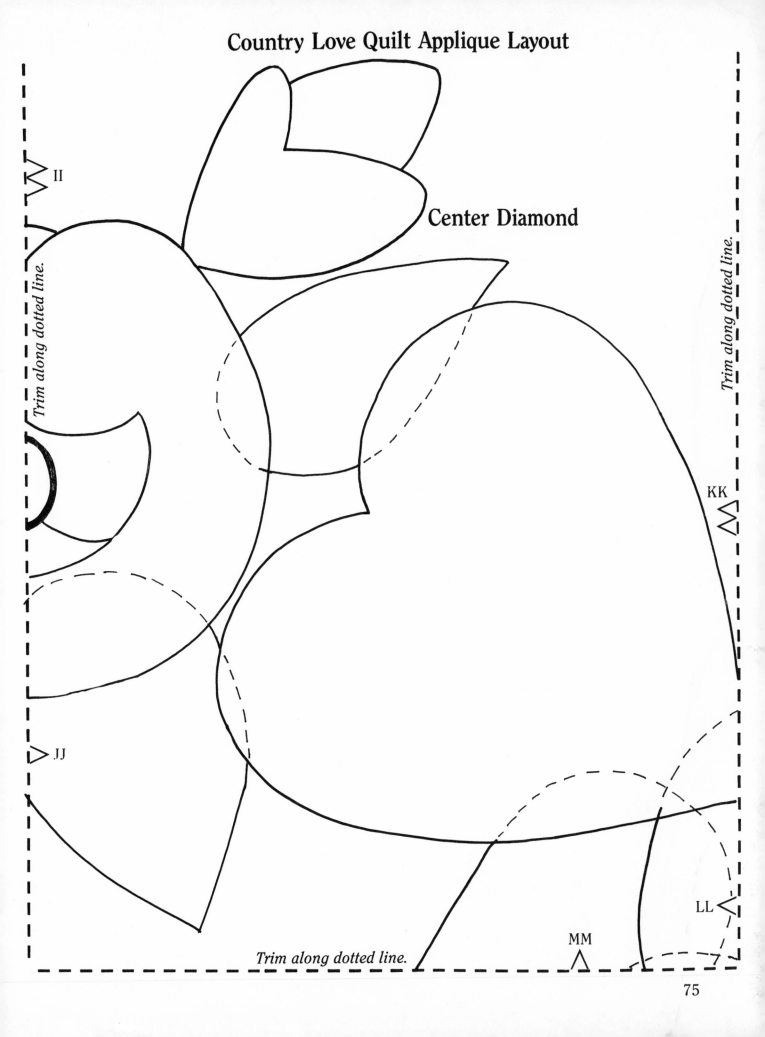

Center Diamond

II

KK

JJ

LL

MM

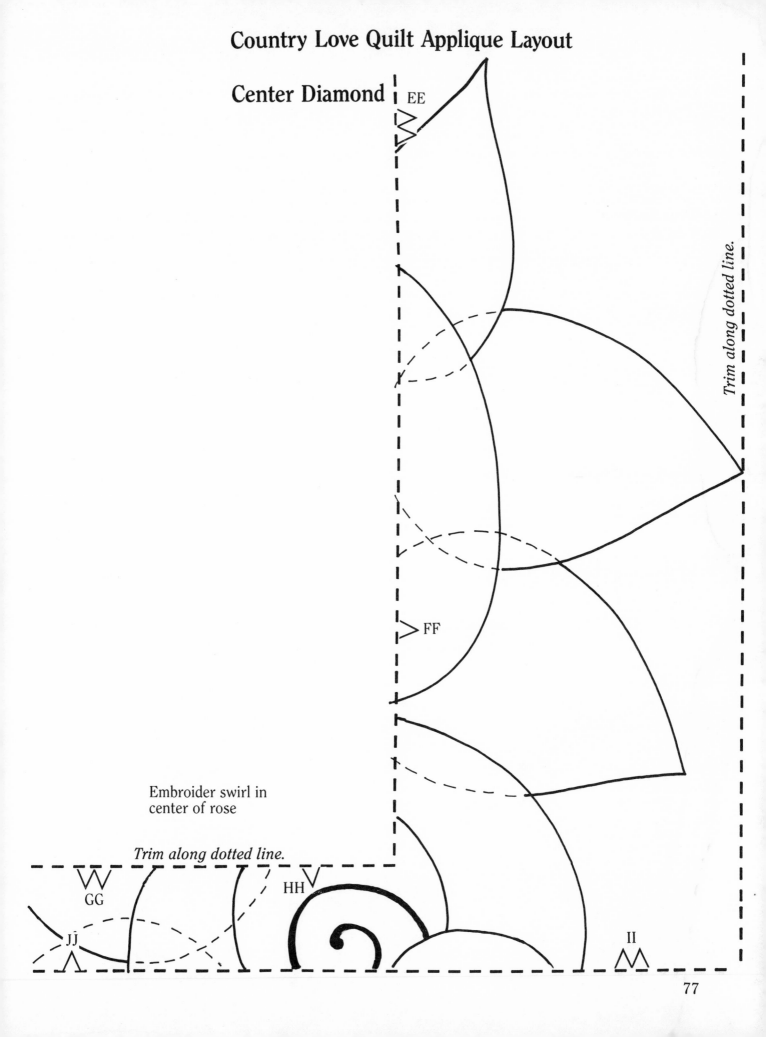

Country Love Quilt Applique Layout

Center Diamond

EE

Trim along dotted line.

FF

Embroider swirl in
center of rose

Trim along dotted line.

GG

HH

JJ

II

EE

CC

Trim along dotted line.

DD

Embroider swirl in
center of roses.

FF

Trim along dotted line.

GG

HH

Country Love Quilt Applique Layout

Trailing Vine

Leaf E

Embroider swirl in center of rose.

Leaf D

←Stem

Trim along dotted line.

K

L

Embroider stem of vine. To create the trailing vine, match corresponding letters and notches along dotted line and tape. Completed Applique layout will look like this:

Country Love Quilt Applique Layout
Trailing Vine

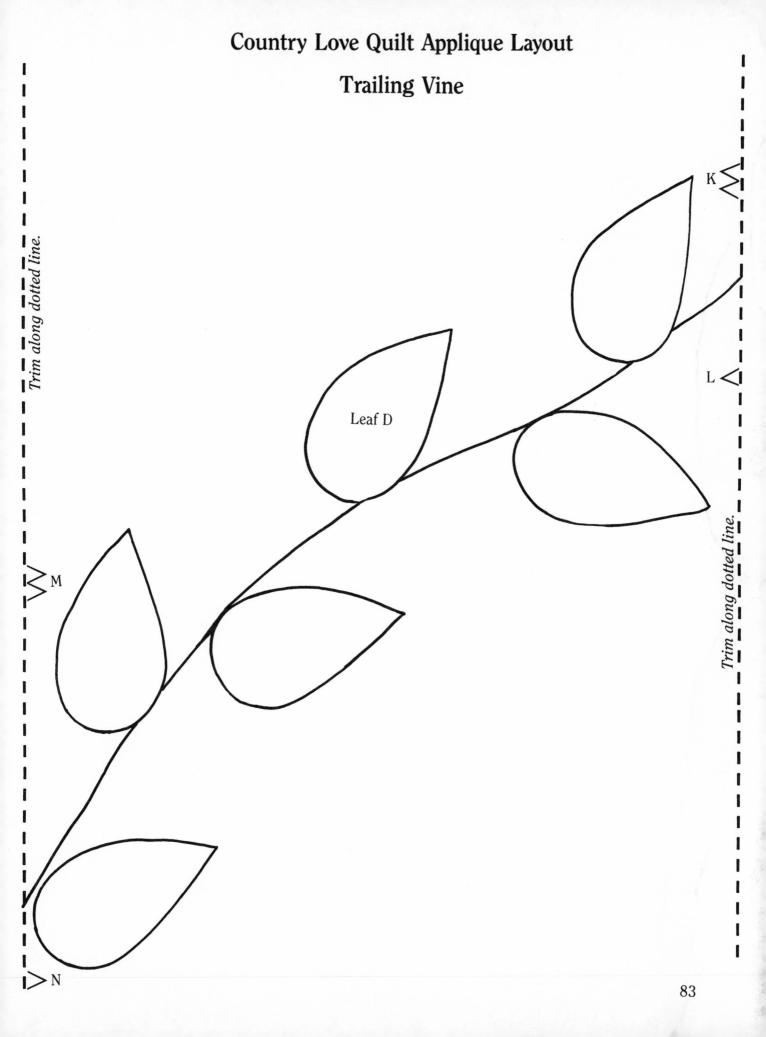

Country Love Quilt Applique Layout
Trailing Vine

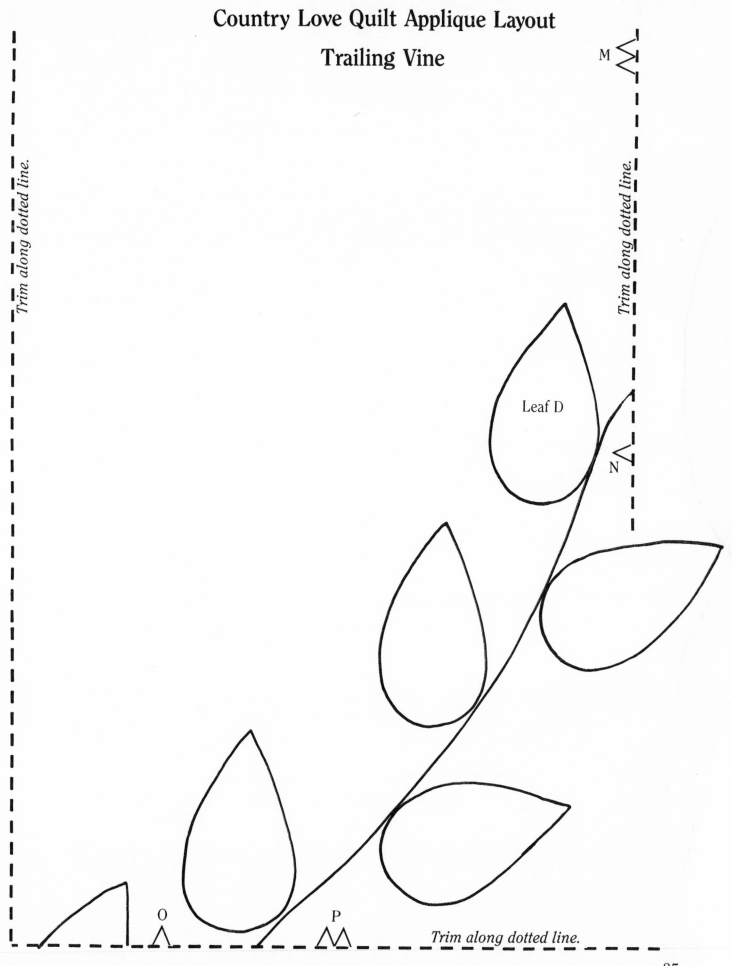

Country Love Quilt Applique Layout
Trailing Vine

Trim along dotted line.

O

P

Leaf D

Q

R

Trim along dotted line.

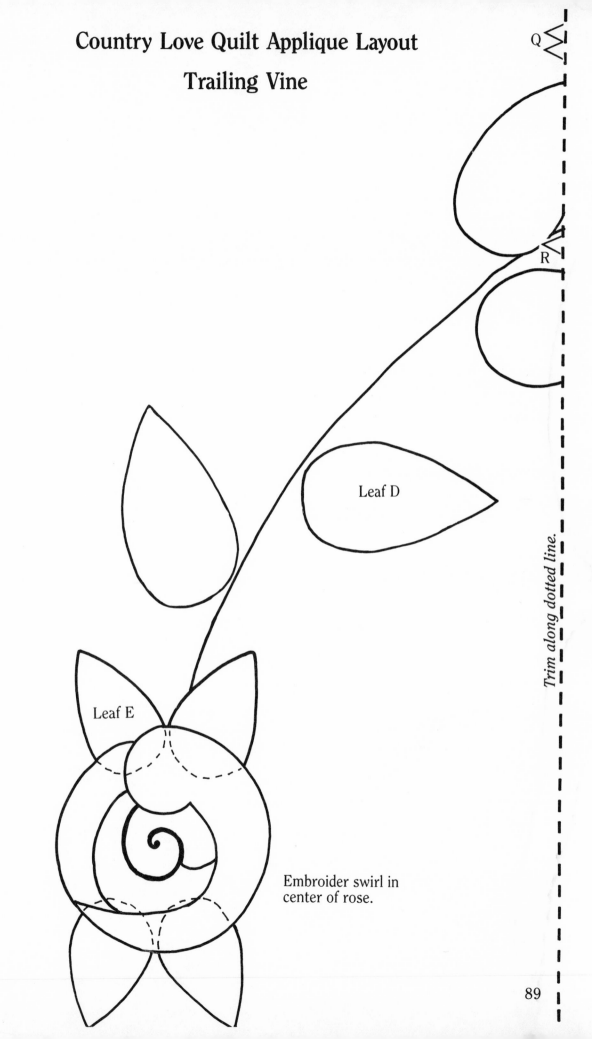

Q

R

Leaf D

Leaf E

Embroider swirl in
center of rose.

Trim along dotted line.

Country Love Quilt Applique Layout

Trim along dotted line.

W S

Add Embroidered swirl here to complete the Pillow Throw Section only.

T

Embroider swirl in center of roses

Pillow Throw/Corner Triangle

To create the finished outline, match corresponding letters and notches along dotted lines and tape. Completed Applique layout will look like this:

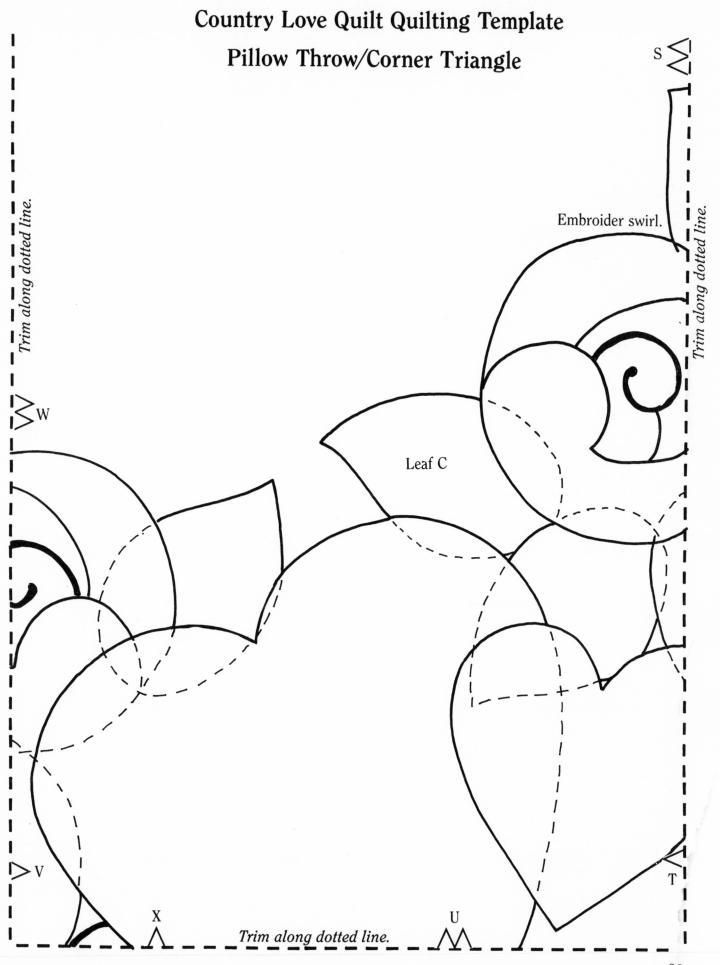

Embroider swirl.

Leaf C

Trim along dotted line.

Trim along dotted line.

Trim along dotted line.

S

W

V

X

U

T

Country Love Quilt Applique Layout

Add Embroidered swirl here to complete the Pillow Throw Section only.

W

Pillow Throw/Corner Triangle

Embroider swirl in center of roses

V

Trim along dotted line.

Embroider swirl.

X

U

95

Country Love Quilt Applique Layout

Embroider swirl

Leaf C

Leaf D

Pillow Throw

Add embroidered lines and the
3 additional leaves on both sides.
Completed Pillow Throw layout will
look like this:

Country Love Quilt Quilting Template
Pillow Throw Border of Quilted Hearts

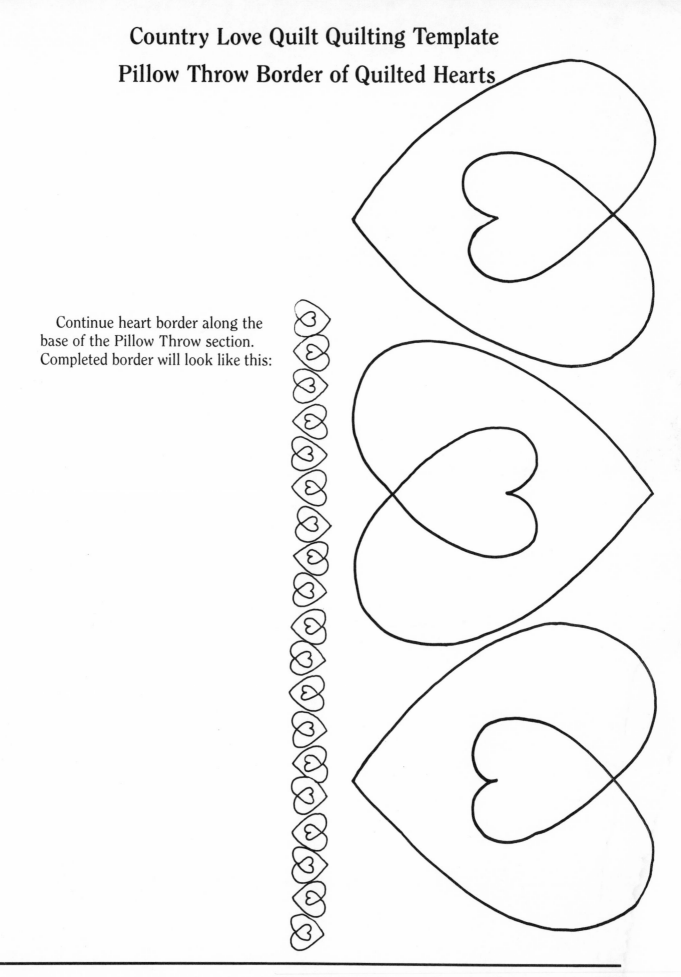

Continue heart border along the base of the Pillow Throw section. Completed border will look like this:

Trim along dotted line.

W
F

V
E

Quilted Feather Chain

Connect corresponding letters
and notches along dotted lines and
tape. Completed layout will look
like this.

Country Love Quilt Quilting Template
Quilted Feather Chain

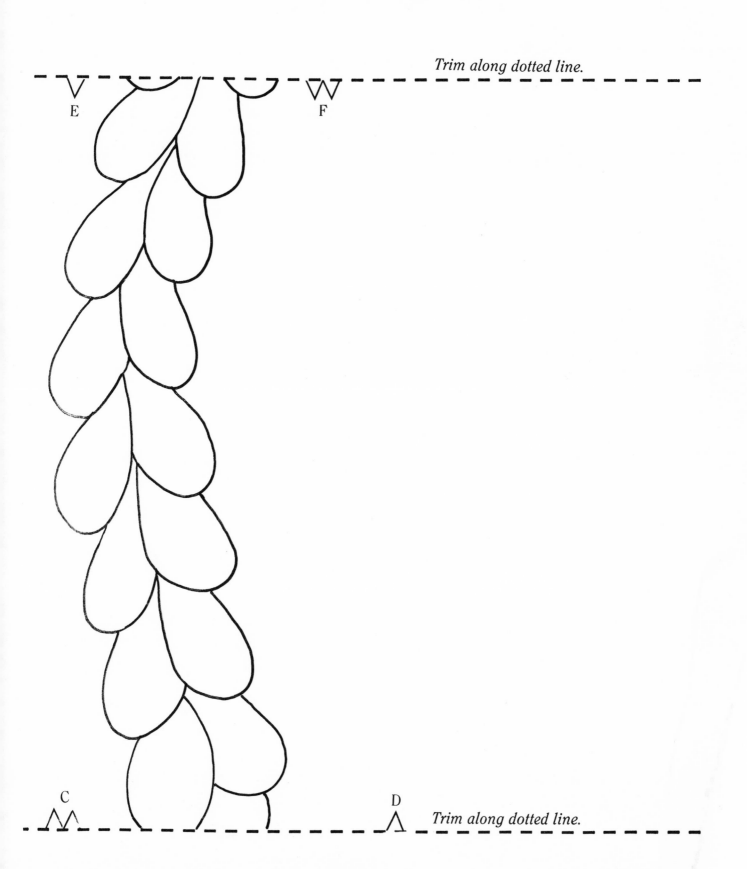

Trim along dotted line.

E   F

C   D *Trim along dotted line.*

Country Love Quilt Quilting Template

Quilted Feather Chain

Trim along dotted line.

Trim along dotted line.

Quilted Feather Chain

Country Love Quilt Quilting Template

Feather Heart

Trim along dotted line.

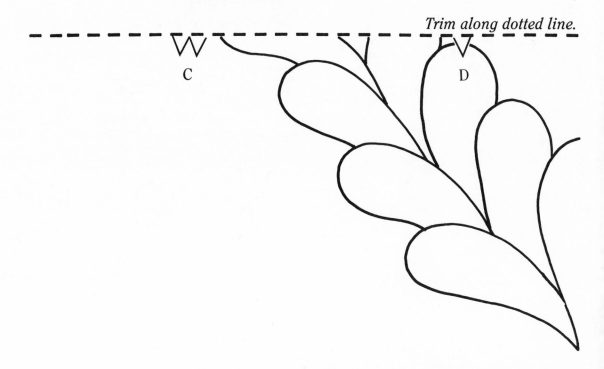

C   D

Connect corresponding letters and notches along dotted lines and tape.   Flop feather heart template to create the other half. Completed template will look like this:

Country Love Quilt Quilting Template
Feather Heart

C

D

Trim along dotted line.

Country Love Quilt Quilting Template

This group of quilted roses appears
in each of the 4 corners
of the center diamond section.

Country Love Quilt Quilting Template
Corner Triangle Bow

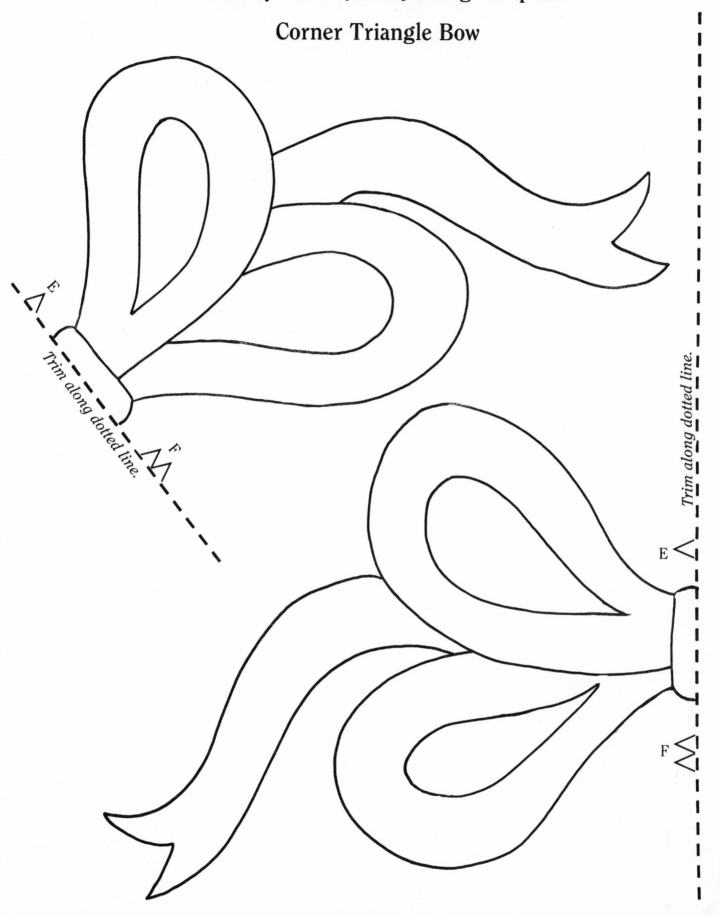

115

The Country Bouquet Quilt
Cutting Lay-out for Queen-size or Double-size Quilt

Final size—approximately 93″ × 109″
Measurements include seam allowances

Total yardage for quilt top—8⅞ yards
Total yardage for quilt back—6¼ yards,
plus 12″ left from cutting side borders.
*For King-size quilt, add enough yardage
to cut 3 additional 20″ patches.*

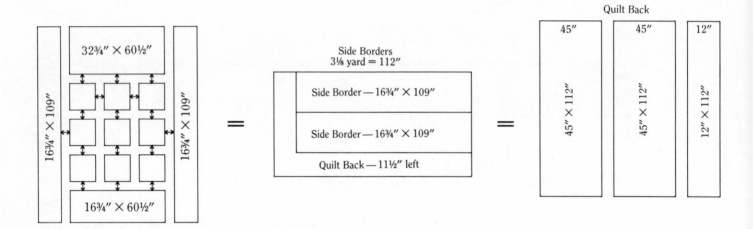

The Country Bouquet Quilt

Assembly Instructions for the Country Bouquet Quilt

Queen-size/Double-size

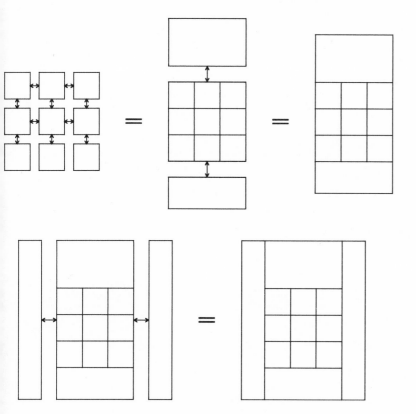

Country Bouquet Quilt Applique Templates

Yardage for Applique

Back Panel of Tulip A and B: ⅜ yard

Front Panel of Tulip A and B: ¼ yard

Leaves: (solid fabric) ½ yard
(print fabric) ½ yard

Outer Hearts: ¼ yard

Inner Hearts: ¼ yard

Fan Flower: ⅛ yard

Fan Flower Base: ⅛ yard

Daisy: ¼ yard

Daisy Center: ⅛ yard

Top of Tulip A and B: ⅛ yard

Tulip Center: ⅛ yard

Bias Tape: Used for vine

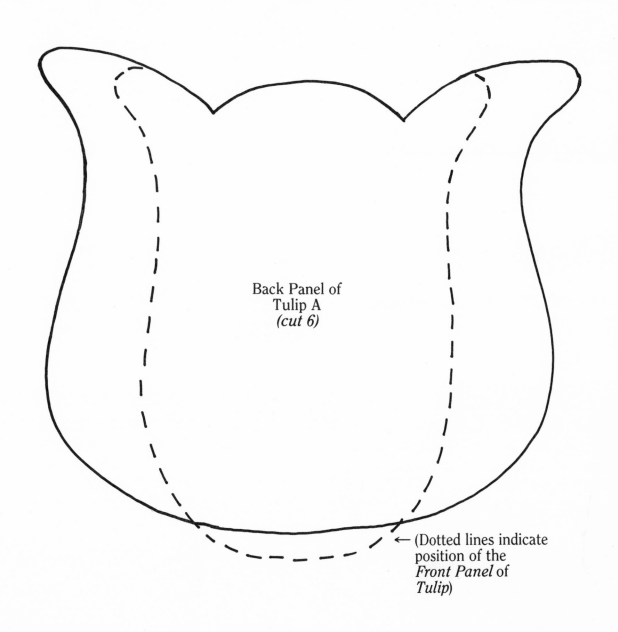

Back Panel of
Tulip A
(cut 6)

← (Dotted lines indicate
position of the
Front Panel of
Tulip)

Country Bouquet Quilt Applique Templates

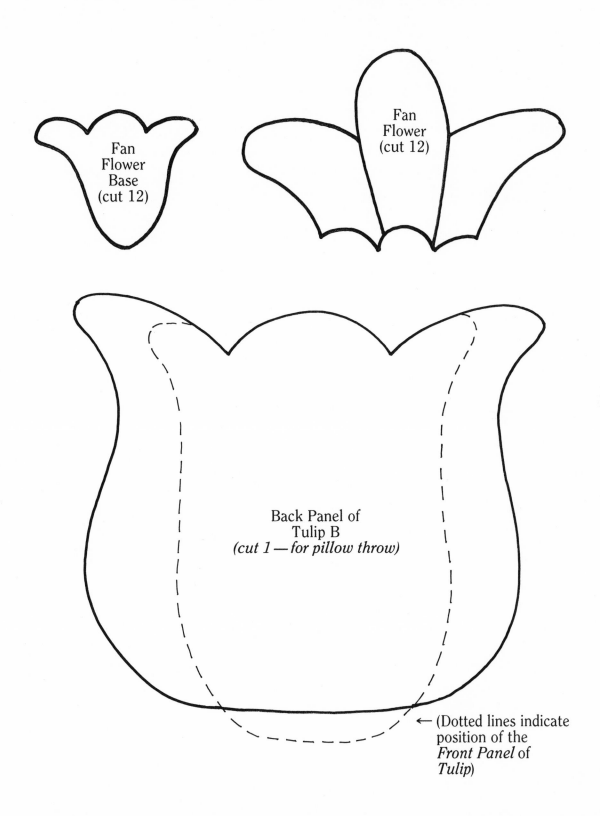

Fan
Flower
Base
(cut 12)

Fan
Flower
(cut 12)

Back Panel of
Tulip B
(cut 1 — for pillow throw)

← (Dotted lines indicate
position of the
Front Panel of
Tulip)

Country Bouquet Quilt Applique Templates

Daisy
(cut 19)

Leaf B
(cut 96)

Daisy
Center
(cut 19)

Outer Heart

(cut 36 of each heart.)

Leaf A
(cut 18)

Inner Heart

Country Bouquet Quilt Applique Templates

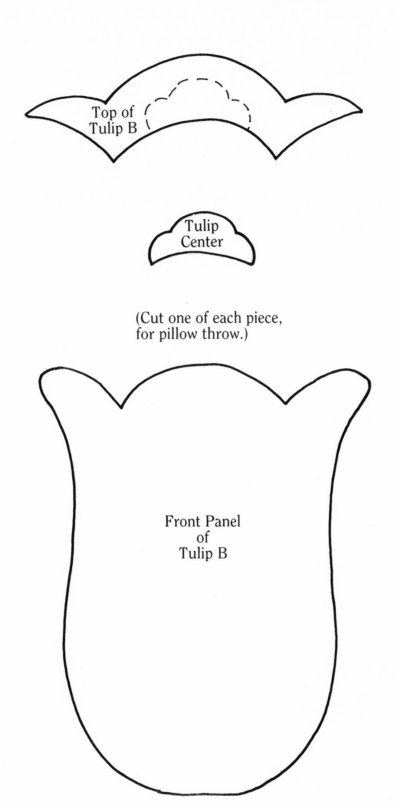

Top of
Tulip B

Tulip
Center

(Cut one of each piece,
for pillow throw.)

Front Panel
of
Tulip B

Country Bouquet Quilt Applique Templates

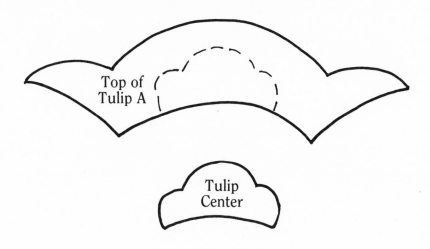

Top of
Tulip A

Tulip
Center

(Cut six of each piece.)

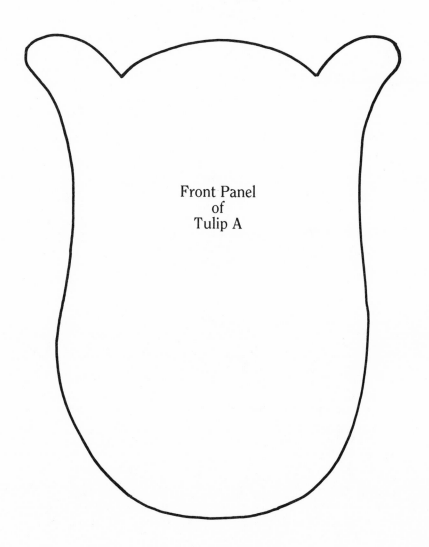

Front Panel
of
Tulip A

Country Bouquet Quilt Applique Layout

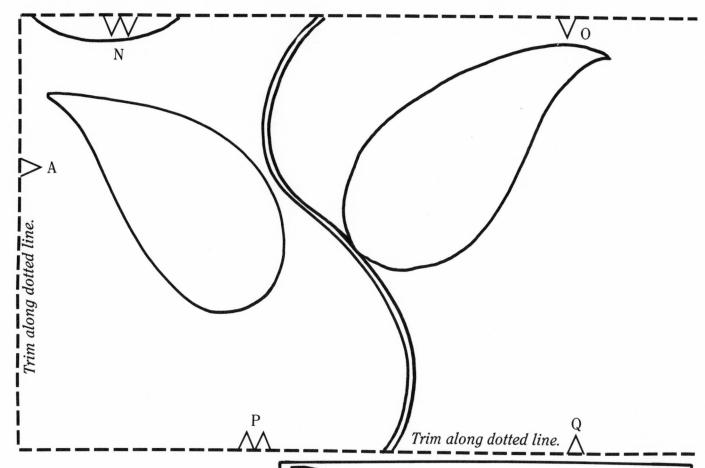

Trim along dotted line.

N

A

Trim along dotted line.

P

Q

To create the finished outline, match corresponding letters and notches and tape. Completed Applique layout will look like this:

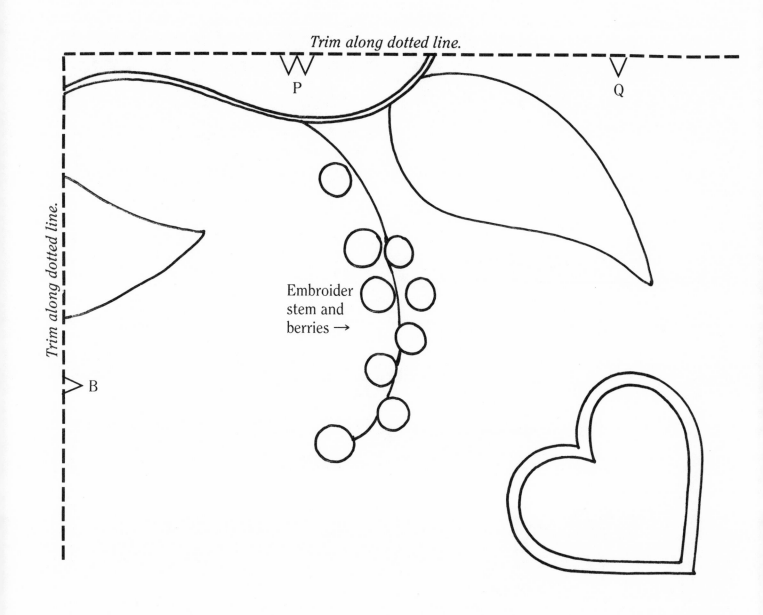

Trim along dotted line.

Trim along dotted line.

P

Q

B

Embroider
stem and
berries →

Trim along dotted line.

M

L

Embroider →
Swirl

←Embroider
Swirl and Vine
Vine can be made
with narrow bias tape,
or embroidered wide.

K

N

O

Country Bouquet Quilt Applique Layout

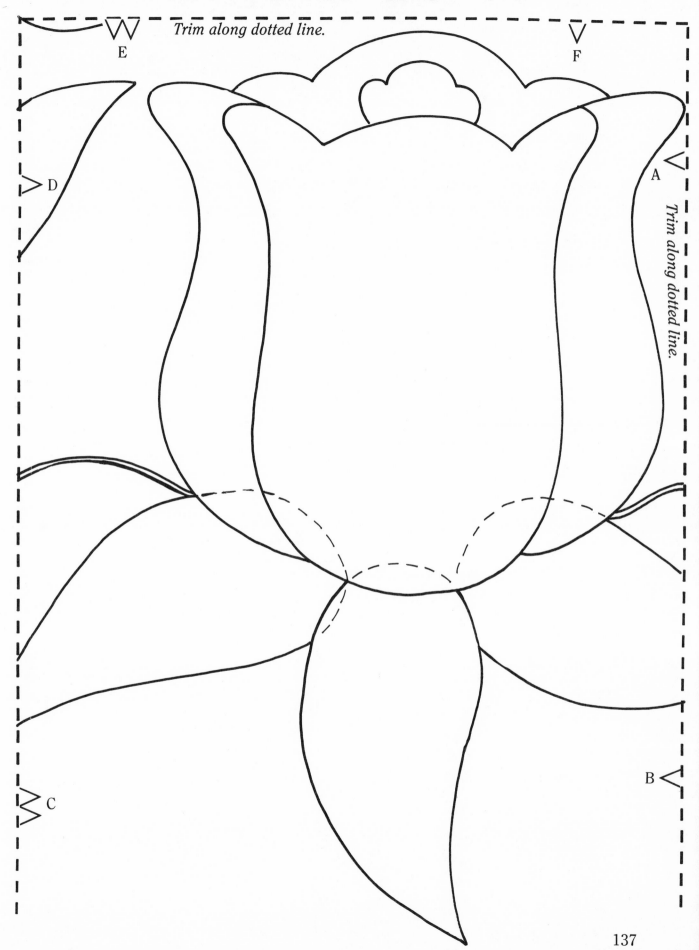

Trim along dotted line.

E

F

Trim along dotted line.

D

A

C

B

Country Bouquet Quilt Applique Layout

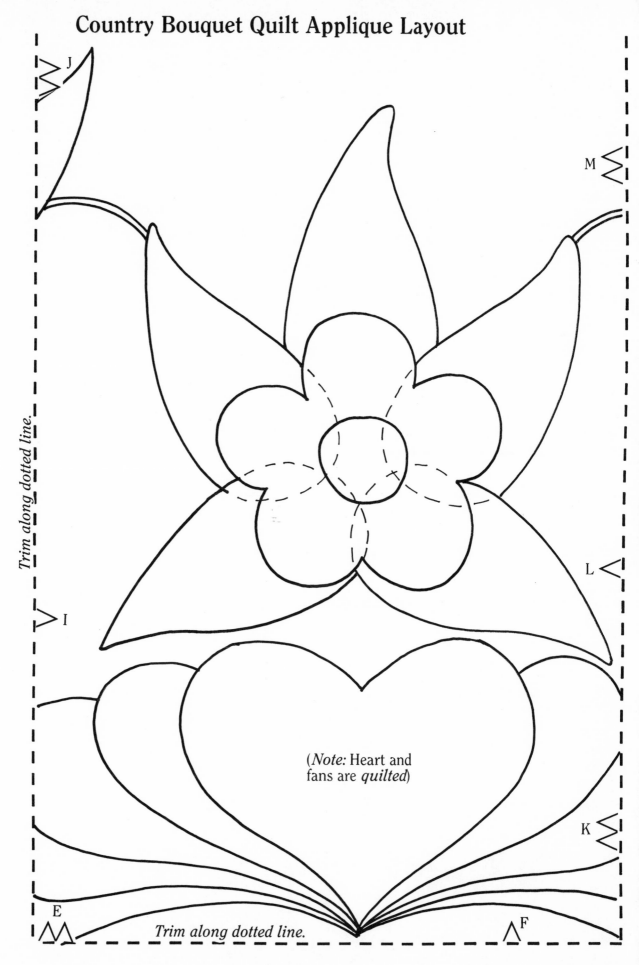

Trim along dotted line.

J

M

L

I

(*Note:* Heart and fans are *quilted*)

K

E

Trim along dotted line.

F

Country Bouquet Quilt Applique Layout

Country Bouquet Quilt Applique Layout

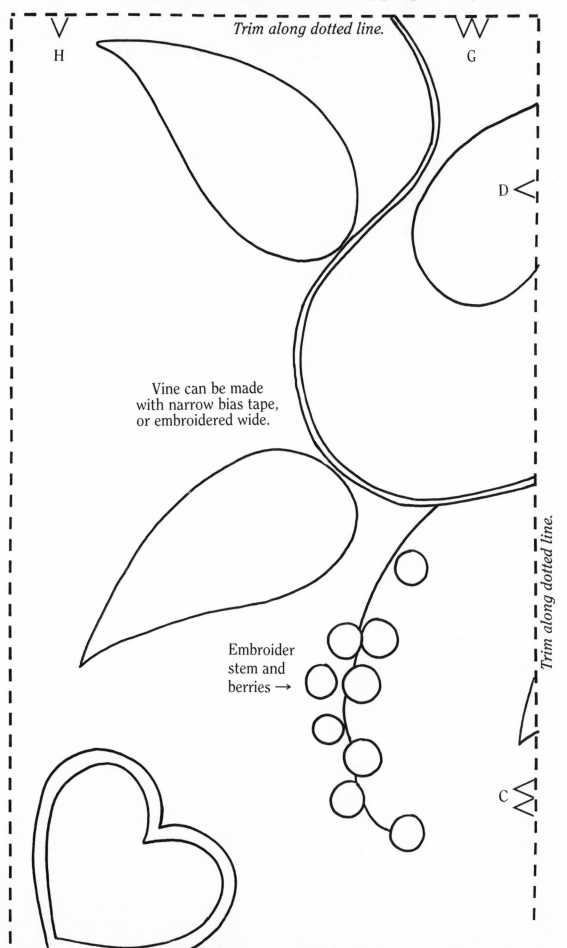

Trim along dotted line.

H

G

D

Vine can be made
with narrow bias tape,
or embroidered wide.

Trim along dotted line.

Embroider
stem and
berries →

C

Country Bouquet Quilt Applique Layout
Pillow Throw

Vine can be made
with narrow bias tape,
or embroidered wide.

To create the finished
outline, match corresponding
letters and notches and tape.
Completed Applique layout
will look like this:

B

A

Trim along dotted line.

Country Bouquet Quilt Applique Layout

Pillow Throw

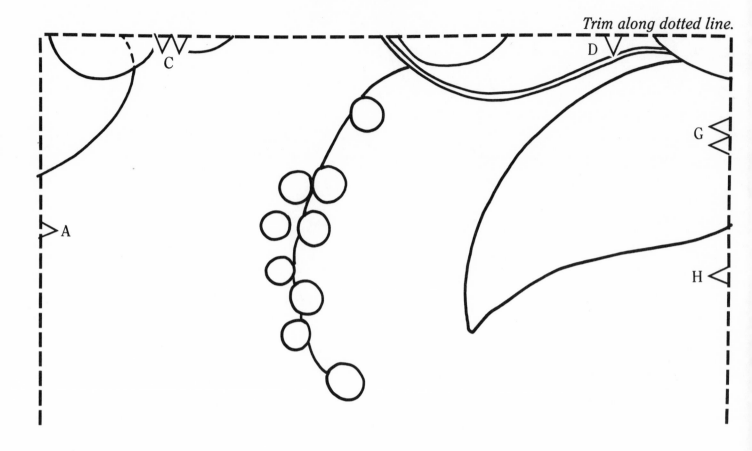

Trim along dotted line.

Trim along dotted line.

Pillow Throw

F

I

E

Trim along dotted line.

G

J

H

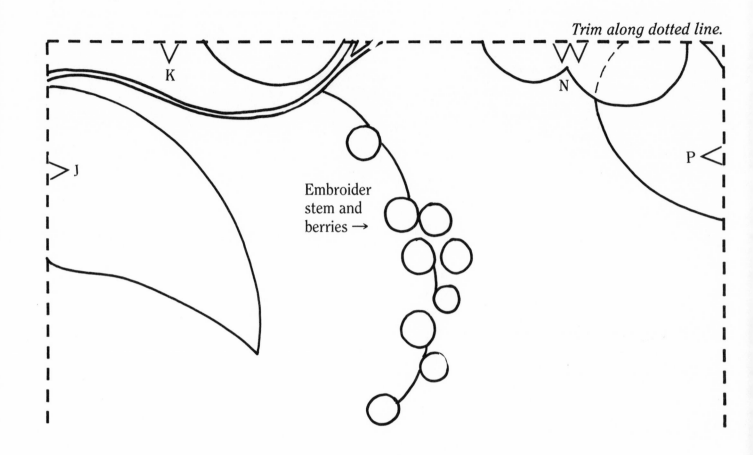

Trim along dotted line.

K

J

Embroider
stem and
berries →

N

W

P

Trim along dotted line.

Trim along dotted line.

L

M

Trim along dotted line.

Vine can be made
with narrow bias tape,
or embroidered wide.

Country Bouquet Quilt Quilting Template

This quilting template completes design on the appliqued patch.

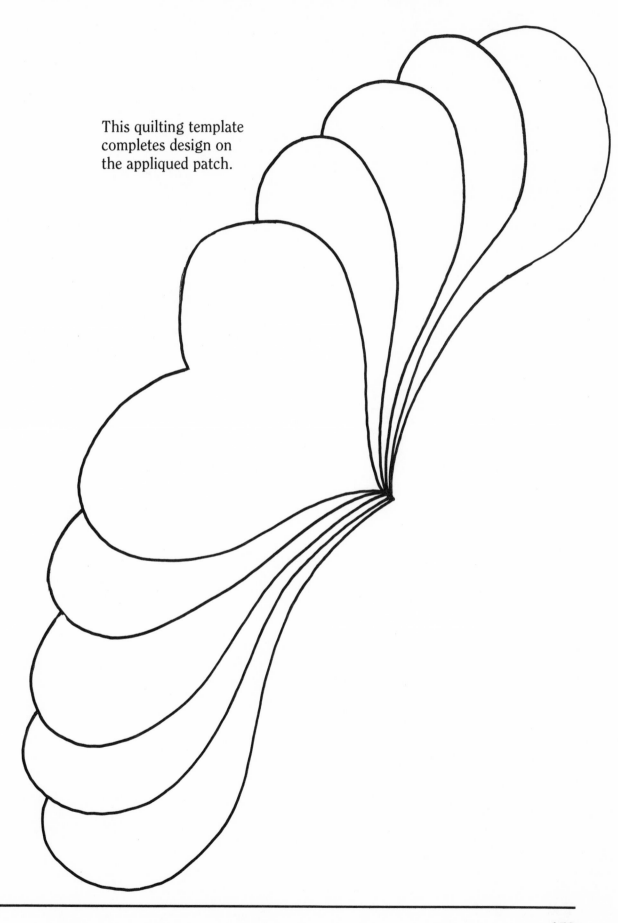

Country Bouquet Quilt
Alternate Patch Quilting Template

To create the finished
outline, match corresponding
letters and notches and tape.
Completed Applique layout
will look like this:

←——— *20″ square* ———→

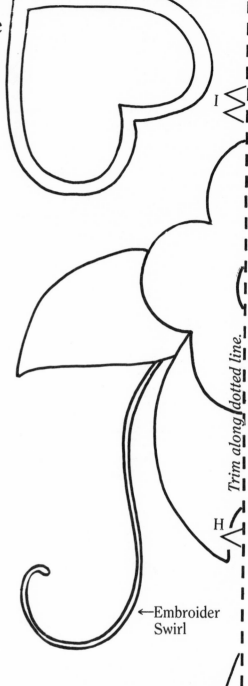

I

Trim along dotted line.

H

←Embroider
Swirl

P

Center line, flop template to create other half of layout.

Country Bouquet Quilt Alternate Patch Quilting Template

Trim along dotted line.

←Embroider
Swirl

Trim along dotted line.

Country Bouquet Quilt Alternate Patch Quilting Template

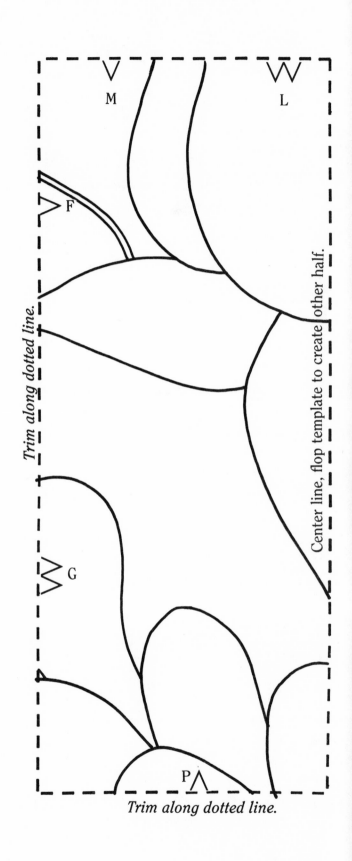

Trim along dotted line.

Center line, flop template to create other half.

Trim along dotted line.

Country Bouquet Quilt Alternate Patch Quilting Template

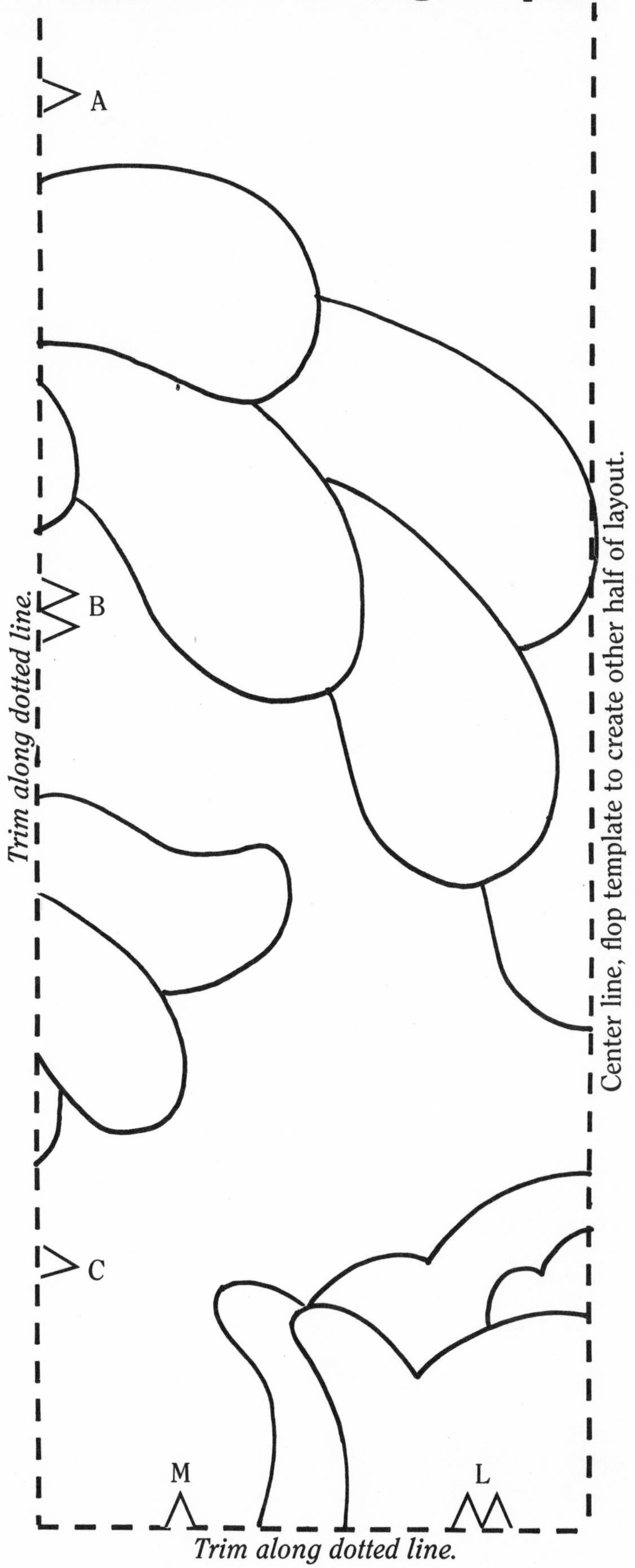

A

B

Trim along dotted line.

C

Center line, flop template to create other half of layout.

M

L

Trim along dotted line.

Country Bouquet Quilt Alternate Patch Quilting Template

A

B

C

D

E

Trim along dotted line.

Country Bouquet Quilt Border Quilting Template

Feather Heart
for Corner Border

Trim along dotted line.

To create the finished
outline, match corresponding
letters and notches and tape.
Completed Applique layout
will look like this:

N

M

G   H

Trim along dotted line.

Country Bouquet Quilt Border Quilting Template

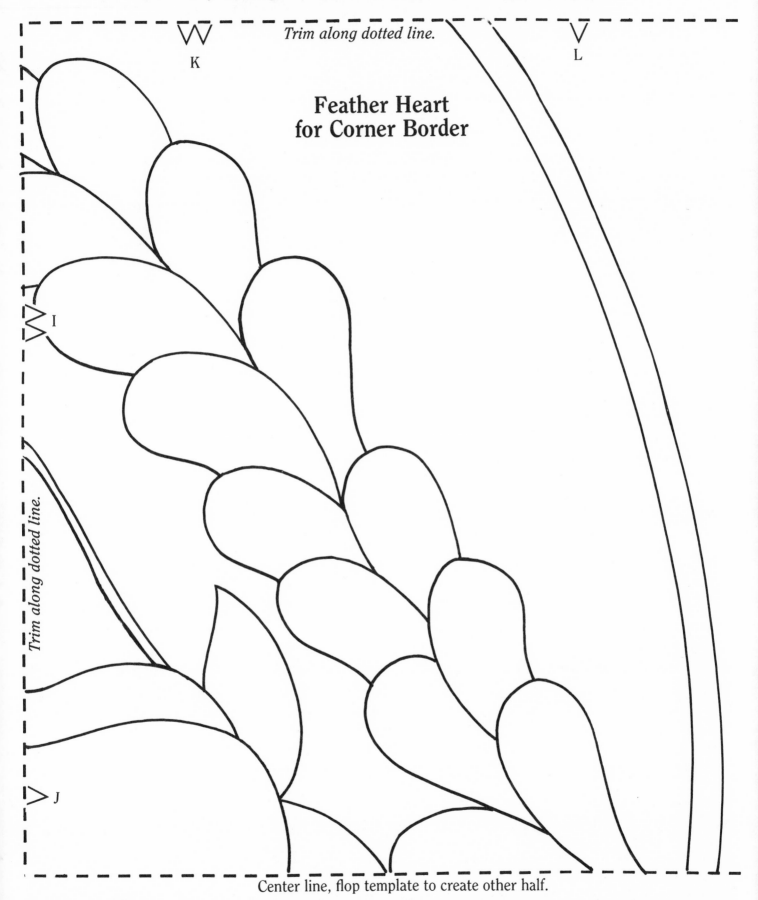

Trim along dotted line.

Feather Heart
for Corner Border

K

L

I

J

Trim along dotted line.

Center line, flop template to create other half.

Country Bouquet Quilt Border Quilting Template

**Feather Heart
for Corner Border**

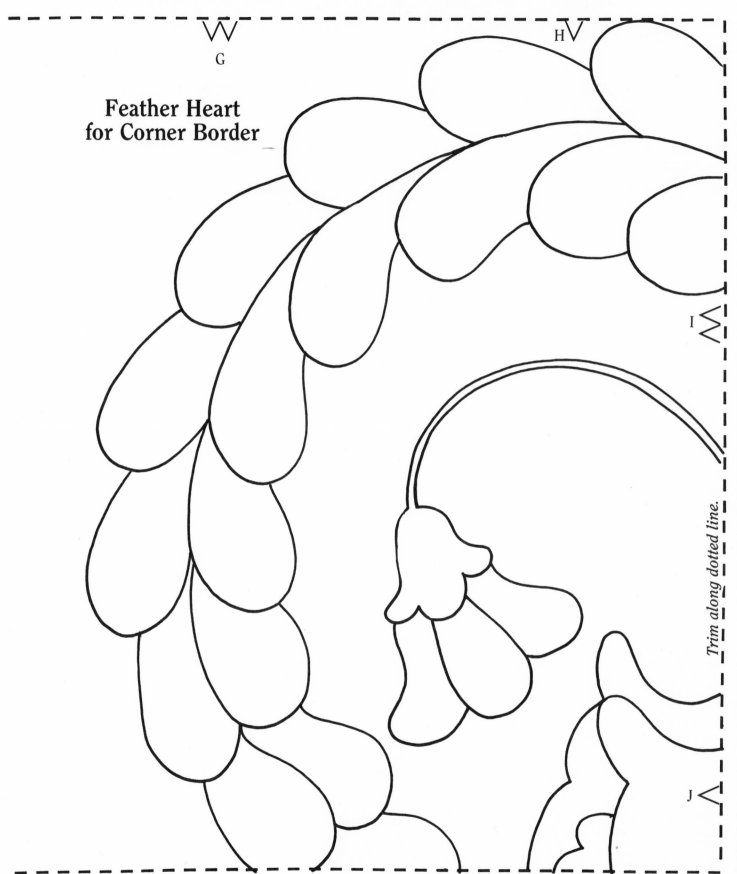

G

H

I

J

Trim along dotted line.

Center line, flop template to create other half of layout.

Feather Heart
for Corner Border

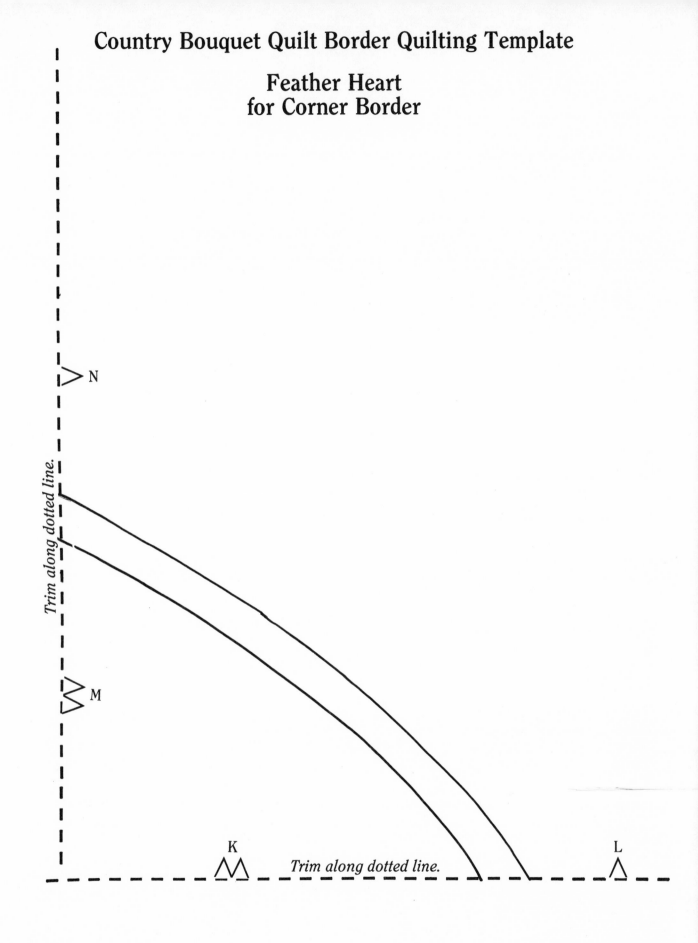

N

Trim along dotted line.

M

K

Trim along dotted line.

L

Country Bouquet Quilt Border Quilting Template

Scallop Border

To create the finished outline, match corresponding letters and notches and tape.

Trim along dotted line.

E

F

Edge of Quilt

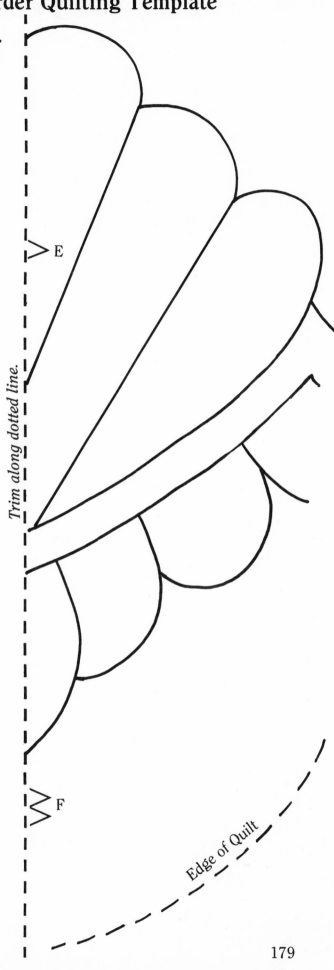

Country Bouquet Quilt Border Quilting Template

Scallop Border

C

E

Trim along dotted line.

Trim along dotted line.

D

Edge of Quilt

F

Country Bouquet Quilt Border
Quilting Template

Scallop Border

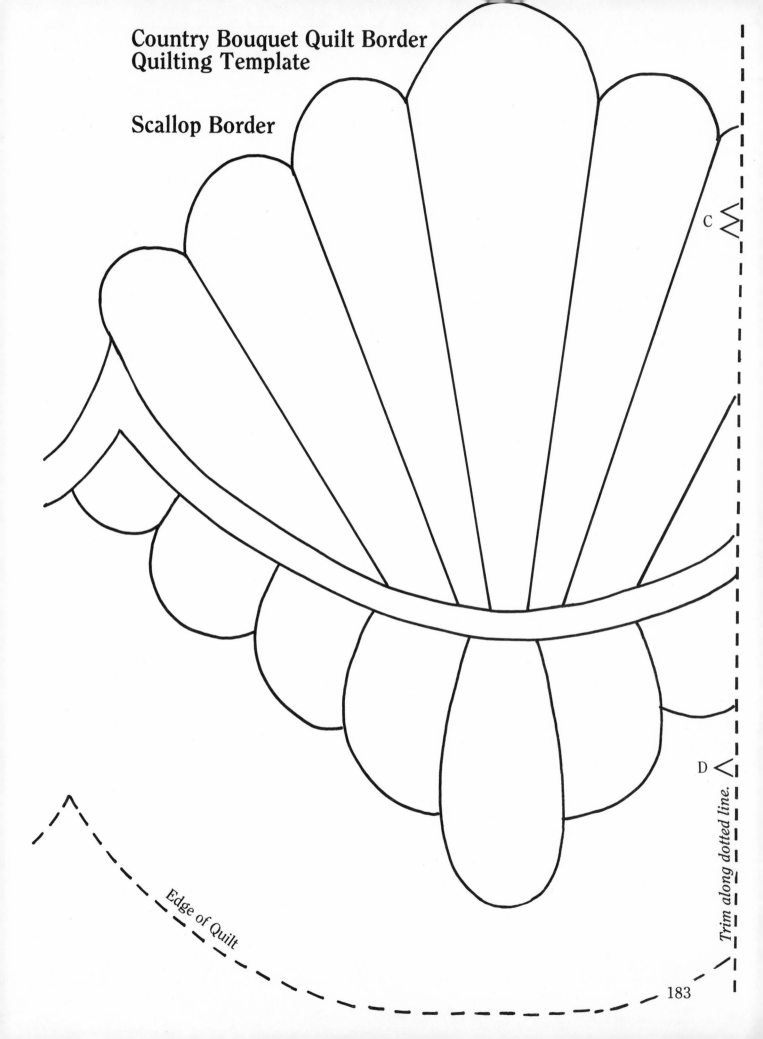

C

D

Trim along dotted line.

Edge of Quilt

183

Country Bouquet Quilt Border Quilting Template

Flower Chain

Trim along dotted line.

Continue quilted flower chain, with the flower above each scallop. See layout.

To create the finished outline, match corresponding letters and notches and tape.

Trim along dotted line.　A　B

Order Form

(all books are paperback)

Quantity

_____ copies of *The Country Love Quilt* @ $12.95 each = $ _____

_____ copies of *The Country Bride Quilt* @ $12.95 each =   _____

_____ copies of *Amish Quilt Patterns* @ $10.95 each =   _____

_____ copies of *Small Amish Quilt Patterns* @ $10.95 each =   _____

_____ copies of *Making Animal Quilts: Patterns and Projects* @ $10.95 each =   _____

_____ copies of *Patterns for Making Amish Dolls and Doll Clothes* @ $12.95 each =   _____

Subtotal $ _____

PA residents add 6% sales tax _____

Shipping and handling (Add 5%, $1.50 minimum) _____

TOTAL $ _____

METHOD OF PAYMENT

☐ Check or Money Order (payable to Good Books in U.S. funds)

☐ Please charge my:

   ☐ MasterCard   ☐ Visa

\# _____ _____ _____ _____ exp. date _____

Signature _____

Name _____

Name _____

Address _____

City _____ State ____ Zip _____

Telephone (_____) _____

SHIP TO: (if different)

Name _____

Address _____

City _____ State ____ Zip _____

Telephone (_____) _____

Mail order to **Good Books,** Main Street, Intercourse, PA 17534; Or call 1-800-762-7171 (in PA and Canada, call collect 717/768-7171).

(Prices subject to change without notice.)

About The
Old Country Store

Cheryl A. Benner and Rachel T. Pellman are on the staff of
The Old Country Store, located along Route 340 in Intercourse,
Pennsylvania. The Store offers crafts from more than 300 arti-
sans, most of whom are local Amish and Mennonites. There are
quilts of traditional and contemporary designs, patchwork
pillows and pillow kits, afghans, stuffed animals, dolls, table-
cloths and Christmas tree ornaments. Other handcrafted items
include potholders, sunbonnets and wooden toys.

For the do-it-yourself quilter, the Store offers quilt supplies,
fabric at discount prices, and a large selection of quilt books and
patterns.

Located on the second floor of the Store is The People's Place
Quilt Museum. The Museum, which opened in 1988, features
antique Amish quilts and crib quilts, as well as a small collection
of dolls, doll quilts, socks and other decorative arts.

About The Authors

Cheryl A. Benner and Rachel T. Pellman together developed The Country Love Quilt and The Country Bouquet Quilt. They selected fabrics and supervised the creation of the original quilts which were made by Lancaster County Mennonite women.

Benner and her husband Lamar live in Honeybrook, Pennsylvania. She is a graduate of the Art Institute of Philadelphia, Philadelphia, Pa. Benner is art director for Good Enterprises, Intercourse, Pa.

Pellman lives in Lancaster, Pa., and is manager of The Old Country, Intercourse. She is co-author of *The Country Bride Quilt.*

She is also the author of *Amish Quilt Patterns* and *Small Amish Quilt Patterns;* co-author with Jan Steffy of *Patterns for Making Amish Dolls and Doll Clothes;* and co-author with her husband, Kenneth, of *The World of Amish Quilts, Amish Crib Quilts,* and *Amish Doll Quilts, Dolls, and Other Playthings.*

The Pellmans are the parents of two sons.